I0464342

OIL AND GAS ACTIVITIES WITH-IN THE NATIONAL WILDLIFE REFUGE SYSTEM AND THE FISH AND WILDLIFE SERV-ICE'S INTEREST IN FURTHER REGULATING THEM

OVERSIGHT HEARING

BEFORE THE

SUBCOMMITTEE ON FISHERIES, WILDLIFE, OCEANS AND INSULAR AFFAIRS

OF THE

COMMITTEE ON NATURAL RESOURCES
U.S. HOUSE OF REPRESENTATIVES

ONE HUNDRED THIRTEENTH CONGRESS

SECOND SESSION

Tuesday, May 20, 2014

Serial No. 113–72

Printed for the use of the Committee on Natural Resources

Available via the World Wide Web: http://www.fdsys.gov
or
Committee address: http://naturalresources.house.gov

U.S. GOVERNMENT PUBLISHING OFFICE

88–011 PDF   WASHINGTON : 2015

COMMITTEE ON NATURAL RESOURCES

DOC HASTINGS, WA, *Chairman*
PETER A. DeFAZIO, OR, *Ranking Democratic Member*

Don Young, AK
Louie Gohmert, TX
Rob Bishop, UT
Doug Lamborn, CO
Robert J. Wittman, VA
Paul C. Broun, GA
John Fleming, LA
Tom McClintock, CA
Glenn Thompson, PA
Cynthia M. Lummis, WY
Dan Benishek, MI
Jeff Duncan, SC
Scott R. Tipton, CO
Paul A. Gosar, AZ
Raúl R. Labrador, ID
Steve Southerland, II, FL
Bill Flores, TX
Jon Runyan, NJ
Markwayne Mullin, OK
Steve Daines, MT
Kevin Cramer, ND
Doug LaMalfa, CA
Jason T. Smith, MO
Vance M. McAllister, LA
Bradley Byrne, AL

Eni F. H. Faleomavaega, AS
Frank Pallone, Jr., NJ
Grace F. Napolitano, CA
Rush Holt, NJ
Raúl M. Grijalva, AZ
Madeleine Z. Bordallo, GU
Jim Costa, CA
Gregorio Kilili Camacho Sablan, CNMI
Niki Tsongas, MA
Pedro R. Pierluisi, PR
Colleen W. Hanabusa, HI
Tony Cárdenas, CA
Jared Huffman, CA
Raul Ruiz, CA
Carol Shea-Porter, NH
Alan S. Lowenthal, CA
Joe Garcia, FL
Matt Cartwright, PA
Katherine M. Clark, MA
Vacancy

Todd Young, *Chief of Staff*
Lisa Pittman, *Chief Legislative Counsel*
Penny Dodge, *Democratic Staff Director*
David Watkins, *Democratic Chief Counsel*

———

SUBCOMMITTEE ON FISHERIES, WILDLIFE, OCEANS AND INSULAR AFFAIRS

JOHN FLEMING, LA, *Chairman*
GREGORIO KILILI CAMACHO SABLAN, CNMI, *Ranking Democratic Member*

Don Young, AK
Robert J. Wittman, VA
Glenn Thompson, PA
Jeff Duncan, SC
Steve Southerland, II, FL
Bill Flores, TX
Jon Runyan, NJ
Vance M. McAllister, LA
Bradley Byrne, AL
Doc Hastings, WA, *ex officio*

Eni F. H. Faleomavaega, AS
Frank Pallone, Jr., NJ
Madeleine Z. Bordallo, GU
Pedro R. Pierluisi, PR
Carol Shea-Porter, NH
Alan S. Lowenthal, CA
Joe Garcia, FL
Peter A. DeFazio, OR, *ex officio*

———

CONTENTS

                                                 Page

Hearing held on Tuesday, May 20, 2014.. 1

Statement of Members:

    Fleming, Hon. John, a Representative in Congress from the State of
        Louisiana 1
        Prepared statement of 2
    Sablan, Hon. Gregorio Kilili Camacho, a Representative in Congress from
        the Commonwealth of the Northern Mariana Islands...................................... 3

Statement of Witnesses:

    Guertin, Steve, Assistant Director, U.S. Fish and Wildlife Service 4
        Prepared statement of 6
    Knudson, Kip, Director of State and Federal Relations, State of Alaska 10
        Prepared statement of 11
    Matson, Noah, Vice President, Defenders of Wildlife 48
        Prepared statement of 50
        Additional testimony submitted for the record 55
    Naatz, Dan, Vice President, Independent Petroleum Association of
        America 33
        Prepared statement of 35
    Powell, J. Davis, Board Member, National Association of Royalty Owners,
        Louisiana Chapter 38
        Prepared statement of 39
    Schutt, Ethan, Senior Vice President, Land and Energy Development,
        Cook Inlet Region, Incorporated 41
        Prepared statement of 43

Additional Material Submitted for the Record:

    Artic Slope Regional Corporation, Letter submitted for the record 67
    Fleming, Hon. John, Letter to Director Daniel Ashe, U.S. Fish and Wild-
        life Service submitted for the record 66
    National Wildlife Refuge, Tables submitted for the record 80
    Questions submitted for the record to U.S. Fish and Wildlife Service 70
    State of Alaska, ANILCA Implementation Program, Letter to U.S. Fish
        and Wildlife Service submitted for the record 76

OVERSIGHT HEARING ON OIL AND GAS ACTIVITIES WITHIN THE NATIONAL WILDLIFE REFUGE SYSTEM AND THE FISH AND WILDLIFE SERVICE'S INTEREST IN FURTHER REGULATING THEM

Tuesday, May 20, 2014
U.S. House of Representatives
Subcommittee on Fisheries, Wildlife, Oceans and Insular Affairs
Committee on Natural Resources
Washington, DC

The subcommittee met, pursuant to notice, at 2:16 p.m., in room 1324, Longworth House Office Building, Hon. John Fleming [Chairman of the Subcommittee] presiding.

Present: Representatives Fleming, Young, Duncan, McAllister; Sablan, Shea-Porter, Lowenthal, and Garcia.

Dr. FLEMING. The subcommittee will come to order. The Chairman notes the presence of a quorum.

STATEMENT OF THE HON. JOHN FLEMING, A REPRESENTATIVE IN CONGRESS FROM THE STATE OF LOUISIANA

Dr. FLEMING. Good afternoon. Today the subcommittee will examine the Fish and Wildlife Service's recent efforts to further regulate oil and gas activities within the National Refuge System.

There are about 1,670 active oil and gas wells within the refuge system. Nearly 70 percent of those wells are located in the State of Louisiana, including two gas wells at the Red River National Wildlife Refuge, in my congressional district.

In the vast majority of cases, these wells existed before the refuge was established. The Fish and Wildlife Service did not acquire the non-Federal mineral rights, and the owners of this subsurface property have every legal right to develop their oil and gas resources. This does not mean, however, that these oil and gas activities are unregulated.

In fact, both the Fish and Wildlife Service in 43 States have oil and gas regulations. In every State in which the Service has identified active and inactive wells, regulations have been adopted which protect the environment and public safety through each stage of the extraction process.

More than a decade ago, the Government Accountability Office told the Fish and Wildlife Service that it needed to better train its staff, improve its data collection efforts, and establish a comprehensive inventory of oil and gas wells and infrastructure on refuge lands. Although the Service has failed to fully implement those recommendations, the agency has skipped ahead to issue an advanced notice of proposed rulemaking that telegraphs their intention to produce a panoply of new Federal regulations.

While no one should be surprised that this administration wants more Federal regulations on our energy industry, it is disappointing that the Fish and Wildlife Service didn't fully implement GAO's recommendations on staffing, data collection, and a nationwide tracking system first, before embarking on the latest regulatory effort.

Nevertheless, since curbing this insatiable regulatory appetite is not likely, I would like to highlight several comments I made in my April 23 letter to Director Dan Ashe.

First, any new Federal regulations must recognize that States are already regulating development, and should have primacy over these oil and gas wells within the refuge system.

Second, the Service should not duplicate functions already conducted by the States.

Third, the Service must not establish unreasonable new fees that would have the effect of denying access to non-Federal minerals legally owned by large and small energy companies.

In addition, it is essential that the Service make it crystal clear that it will honor the private property rights of subsurface mineral owners. To do otherwise is to violate their Fifth Amendment constitutional rights.

Finally, horizontal drilling from private lands to access oil and gas under a refuge should not fall under the Service's jurisdiction, and any future rules should not try to add a new duplicative layer of regulation over these activities. It, frankly, makes little sense to require a private land owner to obtain a bond, Federal permits, or to pay any fees for drilling on their own property. In the unlikely event of a spill, it is these land owners, and not the Federal Government, who will be required to clean up their own property and any adjacent affected lands.

[The prepared statement of Dr. Fleming follows:]

PREPARED STATEMENT OF THE HON. JOHN FLEMING, CHAIRMAN, SUBCOMMITTEE ON FISHERIES, WILDLIFE, OCEANS AND INSULAR AFFAIRS

Good afternoon, today, the subcommittee will examine the Fish and Wildlife Service's recent efforts to further regulate oil and gas activities within the National Wildlife Refuge System.

There are about 1,670 active oil and gas wells within the refuge system. Nearly 70 percent of those wells are located in the State of Louisiana including two gas wells at the Red River National Wildlife Refuge in my Congressional District.

In the vast majority of cases, these wells existed before the refuge was established, the Fish and Wildlife Service did not acquire the non-Federal mineral rights and the owners of this subsurface property have ever legal right to develop their oil and gas resources.

This does not mean, however, that these oil and gas activities are unregulated. In fact, both the Fish and Wildlife Service and 43 States have oil and gas regulations. In every State in which the Service has identified active and inactive wells, regulations have been adopted which protect the environment and public safety through each stage of the extraction process.

More than a decade ago, the Government Accountability Office (GAO) told the Fish and Wildlife Service that it needed to better train its staff, improve its data collection efforts and establish a comprehensive inventory of oil and gas wells and infrastructure on refuge lands.

Although the Service has failed to fully implement those recommendations, the agency has skipped ahead to issue An Advanced Notice of Proposed Rulemaking that telegraphs their intention to produce a panoply of new Federal regulations.

While no one should be surprised that this Administration wants more Federal restrictions on our energy industry, it is disappointing that the Fish and Wildlife Service didn't fully implement GAO's recommendations on staffing, data collection, and a nationwide tracking system first before embarking on this latest regulatory effort.

Nevertheless, since curbing this insatiable regulatory appetite is not likely, I would like to highlight several comments I made in my April 23 letter to Director Dan Ashe. First, any new Federal regulations must recognize that States are already regulating development, and should have primacy over these oil and gas wells within the refuge system.

Second, the Service should not duplicate functions already conducted by the States.

Third, the Service must not establish unreasonable new fees that would have the effect of denying access to non-Federal minerals legally owned by both large and small energy companies.

In addition, it is essential that the Service make it crystal clear that it will honor the private property rights of subsurface mineral owners. To do otherwise, is to violate their 5th Amendment Constitutional rights.

Finally, horizontal drilling from private lands to access oil and gas under a refuge should not fall under the Service's jurisdiction and any future rules should not try to add a new, duplicative layer of regulation over those activities. It frankly makes little sense to require a private landowner to obtain a bond, Federal permits or to pay any fees for drilling on their own property. In the unlikely event of a spill, it is these landowners and not the Federal Government who will be required to clean-up their own property and any adjacent affected lands.

———

Dr. FLEMING. I will now recognize the Ranking Member for any statement he would like to make. I yield to you, Mr. Sablan.

STATEMENT OF THE HON. GREGORIO KILILI CAMACHO SABLAN, A DELEGATE IN CONGRESS FROM THE TERRITORY OF THE NORTHERN MARIANA ISLANDS

Mr. SABLAN. Thank you very much, Mr. Chairman. And good afternoon, everyone.

President George Bush created two national wildlife refuges in my district, the Northern Mariana Islands: the Mariana Arc of Fire National Wildlife Refuge and the Marianas Trench National Wildlife Refuge. So, naturally, I am very interested when we have a hearing on our Nation's refuge system.

Of course, I am not alone. We have over 500 wildlife refuges, nationwide. And I think very nearly every Member of Congress has a refuge in their district.

The refuges bring in some big money. They create business opportunities and jobs, they are great for people who like to hunt and fish and enjoy the outdoors. They also cost money to maintain. That is why I introduced legislation in the last Congress to authorize a semi-postal stamp to raise money for upkeep in our refuge. We had 52 Republicans and Democrats sponsor that bill, including yourself, Mr. Chairman. And you were kind enough to hold a hearing and get the bill reported out of the Natural Resources Committee, though it got hung up further down the line.

So, I know that we all share a care about our refuge. And, frankly, I was rather shocked when I started reading through today's testimony, because at the same time that we are trying to raise a little money with efforts like the semi-postal stamp, and save the taxpayers the cost of keeping our refuge clean and beautiful, apparently we have hundreds or thousands of abandoned oil wells out in the refuge that are doing just the opposite. They are costing the taxpayers money, like this one in the St. Catherine Creek National

Wildlife Refuge, just across the border from the Chairman, in Mississippi.

It seems it was improperly plugged and abandoned in 1983 by the private owners. Then, when it started leaking 33 years later, the State of Mississippi said the Federal Government was responsible for the cleanup, to the tune of $260,000. That's $260,000, Mr. Chairman—you will have to sell a lot of semi-postal stamps to make up that kind of money.

So, I guess we are going to hear that St. Catherine Creek is not an isolated example. And so I want to say thank you, again, for holding today's hearing. Any time we uncover a situation where private interest gets the fist and Federal taxpayers get stuck with the bill, then this subcommittee needs to pay attention, and maybe take action.

It looks as though the Fish and' Wildlife Service is ahead of us, though. They have already solicited ideas from 47,000 Americans about how to address this problem, when people leave a mess on our lands and then expect the rest of us to pay for the cleanup. And I understand that the Service will now be going ahead and drafting some proposals on how to get a handle on this problem that is costing taxpayers money, and soiling our wildlife refuge.

I am looking forward to hearing what they have to tell us and all our witnesses. And I yield back the balance of my time. Thank you.

Dr. FLEMING. I thank the gentleman, the Ranking Member, Mr. Sablan.

I will now ask our panel members to come forward, and I will be introducing you while you move forward.

We will hear from Mr. Steve Guertin, Assistant Director, U.S. Fish and Wildlife Service, and Mr. Kip Knudson, Director of State and Federal Relations for the State of Alaska.

Just a reminder, your written testimony will appear in full in the hearing record, so I ask that you keep your oral statements to 5 minutes, as outlined in our invitation letter to you under Committee Rule 4(a).

Our microphones are not automatic. You will need to push the button and make sure the tip is close by to be heard.

The timing lights, very simple. You will be under green light for 4 minutes, yellow light the last minute. And, of course, when the red light comes on, please conclude your comments as quickly as possible. And, again, your full testimony will be in the record.

Mr. Guertin, you are now recognized, sir, for 5 minutes.

STATEMENT OF STEVE GUERTIN, ASSISTANT DIRECTOR, U.S. FISH AND WILDLIFE SERVICE

Mr. GUERTIN. Good afternoon, Chairman Fleming, Ranking Member Sablan, and members of the subcommittee. I am Steve Guertin, Deputy Director for the U.S. Fish and Wildlife Service. We appreciate the opportunity to testify before you today regarding oil and gas development on National Wildlife Refuge System lands, and the Service's interest in ensuring a common-sense, predictable, and consistent approach to regulating development to protect taxpayer investments in the National Wildlife Refuge System.

The Refuge System is the world's premier network of public lands devoted solely to the conservation of wildlife and habitat. It encompasses over 150 million acres of land and water, and preserves a diverse array of land, wetlands, and ocean ecosystems. The Refuge System offers about 47 million visitors a year the opportunity to fish, hunt, observe, and photograph wildlife, as well as learn about nature through environmental education and interpretation. These visitors make refuges an important economic driver, generating nearly $2.4 billion for local economies each year, and supporting over 35,000 jobs. And refuges are a good investment. Each dollar appropriated for the refuge system returns nearly $5 to economic benefits.

A large number of refuges also support varying levels of oil and gas development. This is because subsurface mineral rights of refuges are often held by private parties. The Service recognizes and respects that these private interests are fully entitled to reasonable access to explore and develop, for example, their oil and gas resources. In fact, oil and gas development can be found on over 200 of the Nation's 562 refuges. There are over 5,000 wells and 1,300 miles of pipeline in the refuge system today.

And those numbers are likely to increase. Domestic energy production is rapidly expanding across the country. Recent advances in drilling technology, the refuge system has experienced an unprecedented level of interest in developing formations such as the Marcellus in the eastern United States and the Bakken in North Dakota and Montana, both previously cost-prohibitive.

The Service has successfully worked with oil and gas across the country to facilitate access and development in ways that minimize impacts. However, in many cases, there are instances of oil and gas development that has had some significant impacts to refuges. The impact varies because there is no framework for consistent permitting that minimizes effects through sensible best management practices.

Some examples of impacts include habitat fragmentation from construction of access roads, abandoned infrastructure, oil leaks from wells and storage tanks, and contamination. A long-term concern is the damage that would occur from the degradation of poorly capped and abandoned wells.

To protect the taxpayers' investment and sportsmen's investment in the refuge system, we are considering regulations for the management of non-Federal oil and gas development on Refuge System lands. Such regulations would provide best practices for access, development, and including development. They would also provide private mineral right holders with a consistent and predictable framework.

To pursue this goal, the Service recently announced an advance notice of proposed rulemaking and a notice of intent to prepare an environmental impact statement on non-Federal oil and gas development on Refuge System lands. Based on the volume of comments, request for an extension on this process, and our desire to continue to work with stakeholders, we plan to reopen this for an additional 30-day comment period next week.

The ANPR provides an opportunity for the Service to meet with stakeholders, including oil and gas operators, conservation groups,

Tribes, and States, and others, to include their expertise and comments early on in our rulemaking process. This is an optional step, but we believe that involving the public at every start will be critical to a more effective rulemaking process and product. Throughout the process we are committed to transparency and public engagement.

Mr. Chairman, you submitted comments to the Service through the ANPR. I have read those comments and have them with me today, and want you to know that we will work with your staff to fully consider your comments, and we will meet with your staff in the future to discuss them as we move forward with the process.

Our mission, as an agency, is working with others to conserve, protect, and enhance fish, wildlife, and plants, and their habitats for the continuing benefit of the American people. We look forward to working with this subcommittee and our stakeholders as we move forward with this process.

Thank you for inviting the Service to testify with you today. We would be happy to answer your questions during the hearing, and we look forward to working with you and the other leaders in Congress and our stakeholders in the future. Thank you.

[The prepared statement of Mr. Guertin follows:]

PREPARED STATEMENT OF STEVE GUERTIN, DEPUTY DIRECTOR, U.S. FISH AND WILDLIFE SERVICE, DEPARTMENT OF THE INTERIOR

Good afternoon Chairman Fleming, Ranking Member Sablan, and members of the subcommittee, I am Steve Guertin, Deputy Director for the U.S. Fish and Wildlife Service (Service) within the Department of the Interior. I appreciate the opportunity to testify before you today regarding oil and gas activities on National Wildlife Refuge System (Refuge System) lands and the Service's interest in ensuring a predictable and consistent approach to regulating that development and protecting taxpayer investments in the Refuge System.

NATIONAL WILDLIFE REFUGE SYSTEM

The Refuge System is the world's premiere network of public lands devoted solely to the conservation of wildlife and habitat. The Refuge System, which encompasses over 150 million acres of land and water, preserves a diverse array of land, wetland, and ocean ecosystems—from remote Pacific islands, north to the high arctic of northern Alaska, east to the rugged coastline of Maine and south to the tropical U.S. Virgin Islands. National wildlife refuges are found in every U.S. State. In total, the Refuge System now contains 562 refuges.

The Refuge System offers about 47 million visitors per year the opportunity to fish, hunt, observe and photograph wildlife, as well as learn about nature through environmental education and interpretation. These visitors make refuges an important economic driver, generating nearly $2.4 billion for local economies each year. In Fiscal Year 2011, the Refuge System supported over 35,000 private-sector jobs. Investing in the Refuge System is a sound use of taxpayer dollars as each dollar appropriated for the Refuge System returns nearly $5 in economic benefits. Refuges also provide local communities with other ecosystem services such as improved water quality and access to quality wildlife-dependent recreation. With its widespread presence and history of working with partners, the Refuge System plays a key role in supporting innovative, community-level efforts to conserve outdoor spaces and connect people with nature.

STATE OF OIL AND GAS ACTIVITIES ON REFUGES

There is a long history of private oil and gas development on national wildlife refuges. Service policy is to purchase the minimum interest necessary to accomplish its conservation mission. In many cases, oil and gas production is ongoing at the time of land acquisition making the purchase of the mineral rights prohibitively expensive. Often, the mineral rights have been severed prior to Federal acquisition of the property. In other cases, the property owner sells to the United States, but retains the mineral rights. Consequently, oil and gas development can be found on nearly half of the Nation's 562 refuges. Federal oil and gas leasing is provided only in situations where adjacent non-Federal development drains resources from the Federal mineral estate (50 CFR 29.31).

Over 200 refuges have existing oil and gas infrastructure (e.g., active and inactive wells, pipelines). Of these, 103 refuges, and four Wetland Management Districts have active oil and gas wells. Over 5,000 wells occur on Refuge System lands and almost 1,300 miles of pipelines cross refuge fee-title lands. Of the 5,000 wells, 1,700 are active and the remaining are inactive or of unknown status. The Service is assessing the status of these wells and is finding many have been inactive for years and even decades. The Service is also identifying wells that no longer have responsible parties (i.e., orphaned wells) and is finding there are many of these wells on refuges.

The Service recognizes that private oil and gas rights holders are fully entitled to reasonable access to explore and develop their oil and gas resources. The Service has had many local successes working with oil and gas operators to achieve appropriate resource protections. However, there are many more examples of unnecessary impacts on resources and refuge management. The cost of addressing these impacts is largely borne by State and Federal taxpayers. Examples of these impacts are described in the following two case studies.

CASE STUDY: ST. CATHERINE CREEK NATIONAL WILDLIFE REFUGE

Due to extensive agricultural development and flood control, the hydrology of the Mississippi River and its floodplain was modified resulting in the loss of 20 million acres of bottomland hardwood forests along the Mississippi River. St. Catherine Creek National Wildlife Refuge (Refuge), established in 1990, preserves 24,931 acres of the Mississippi River floodplain 2 miles south of Natchez, Mississippi. Acquisition of the floodplain habitat included remnants of bottomland hardwood forest, fallow fields, cleared land, and cypress swamps.

Mineral rights were excluded from the land purchased for the Refuge and are privately owned. Since the 1950s, numerous oil wells, pipelines, and oil and oilfield brine storage tanks have been located on lands that are now within the Refuge. While there are relatively few active oil and gas wells on the refuge, the Service has used best available data to identify over 500 inactive wells. Many of the inactive wells have not been properly plugged and abandoned. Since the establishment of the refuge, spills, and leaks from oil wells and pipelines have plagued the Refuge.

A leaking oil well discovered by a Refuge law enforcement officer in April 2012 led to an investigation by the Mississippi State Oil and Gas Board and the Mississippi Department of Environmental Quality. A review of the well's history revealed the well was 6,000 feet in depth and had been plugged and abandoned in 1983. Although the well was never properly plugged and abandoned in 1983, the State's policy transferred the responsibility of re-plugging the well and site cleanup to the surface owner, in this case, the Service. The Refuge wildlife officer reported the leaking well to the National Response Center as an oil spill with the potential to reach the Mississippi River. The report initiated a response from the U.S. Coast Guard and the Environmental Protection Agency (EPA). Because of the severity of the leak, EPA took jurisdiction of the site and assumed all costs for plugging the well and site cleanup.

Re-plugging the well required drilling, cementing and testing at a cost of approximately $95,000. Few States have bond requirements that adequately cover the actual costs to re-plug a well. Mississippi requires only a $10,000 bond for a well. Only two States have regulations with a bond amount sufficient to cover the costs for plugging a well of this size and none require posting a bond in the amount to properly reclaim and restore the site.

Site restoration followed completion of the plugging. All surface contaminants were removed from the well site. The site was seeded and covered with mulch to control erosion. Plugging the well, site restoration and vegetation planting cost $260,000. After much work, trees and grasses are finally becoming re-established at the site.

CASE STUDY: LOWER RIO GRANDE NATIONAL WILDLIFE REFUGE

What happens to long-billed curlews, one of North America's most threatened shorebirds, and thousands of migrating geese, ducks and endangered piping plover when oil and gas infrastructure are abandoned to rust and corrode around lakes that are roosting and nesting habitat?

That question faced the Lower Rio Grande Valley National Wildlife Refuge in Texas when the operator of three wells on East Lake abandoned the sites in the early 1990s. The previously privately owned and operated wells had been drilled in

1948 and there was no liable owner to pay for the cost of the cleanup. Before clean-up, the abandoned production facilities, including storage tanks and sections of rust-ed pipe, extended into East Lake, and threatened contamination of the adjacent wetlands that are habitat for endangered piping plover in the winter. They also posed potential health risks to other native wildlife. Oil sheens were visible in East Lake near one of the abandoned wells.

After 15 years of working with the Texas Railroad Commission (TRRC), the State's oil and gas regulatory agency, the TRRC began plugging the wells in June 2011. The cost to taxpayers was approximately $1.2 million to clean up the aban-doned well sites and remove the oil and gas equipment from the refuge.

Transport of cleanup and plugging equipment brought its own set of problems: track buggies, which delivered the equipment, became mired in the lake bed and dug ruts in the substrate. The substrate then had to be restored. Storage tanks, pipes, and other oil production equipment were removed from the three well sites. Metal that could be recycled was taken to a metal salvage yard. Refuge habitat was restored. Immediate plugging and equipment removal would have lessened the costs and impacts to the refuge, State regulatory agencies, and the taxpayers.

NEED FOR REVISED OIL AND GAS REGULATIONS

In order to keep pace with increased development pressure, protect taxpayer in-vestments in the Refuge System, and to bring needed consistency and predictability to the holders of mineral rights in the Refuge System, the Service is considering promulgating regulations for oil and gas operations in the Refuge System. The Service is considering such regulations pursuant to recommendations made by the Government Accountability Office (GAO). Such regulations would be similar to those already in place by other land management agencies.

In 2003 and 2007, the Government Accountability Office (GAO) issued reports to Congress recommending the Service clarify permitting authority for non-Federal oil and gas operations. In the 2003 Report to Congress (GAO–03–517), GAO high-lighted the opportunities to improve management and oversight of oil and gas oper-ations on the Refuge System. One of the main recommendations of the report was to clarify the Service's permitting authority of non-Federal oil and gas operations through regulations. Currently, the primary regulation the U.S. Fish and Wildlife Service uses for management of non-Federal oil and gas development on Refuge Sys-tem lands comes from 50 CFR 29.32. This regulation pertains to non-Federal min-eral rights on Refuge System lands. The current regulation does not provide the Service with adequate authority to ensure the protection of refuge resources. An up-date by GAO in 2007 (GAO–07–829R) followed the 2003 report reasserting the rec-ommendation that the Service take the necessary steps to apply a consistent and reasonable set of regulatory and management controls over oil and gas activities oc-curring on the Refuge System to protect the public's surface interests.

Several other land management agencies have regulations that cover oil and gas development, including the Department of the Interior's National Park Service (NPS) and the U.S. Department of Agriculture's Forest Service (FS). A comprehen-sive and cohesive oil and gas management program for the Service could help achieve an appropriate balance between the Refuge System mission and the reason-able exercise of private oil and gas rights. To that end, the Service is considering a rulemaking for the management of non-Federal oil and gas operations in the Refuge System. The goal of such a regulation would be to achieve the necessary pro-tections for ecosystems and wildlife on refuges while respecting the property rights of the holders of private mineral rights.

On February 24, 2014, the Service announced an Advanced Notice of Proposed Rulemaking (ANPR) and notice of intent to prepare an environmental impact state-ment on Non-Federal Oil and Gas Development on Refuge System Lands. Through this transparent, public process, the Service is seeking public input at the initial stages of the process of considering rulemaking. The ANPR provides us with the op-portunity to meet with stakeholders from the public, oil and gas industry, conserva-tion groups, and tribes to include their expertise and comments as early as possible in the process of considering rulemaking. Working in collaboration with these stake-holders will improve the Service's ability to ensure landscapes are capable of sup-porting sustainable populations of fish and wildlife while also providing for the energy needs of local communities—now and in the future.

A fundamental aspect of a new rule could be to improve regulatory consistency to the benefit of both refuge managers and oil and gas operators. Regulations should be standards-based as opposed to prescriptive. Both resource managers and project proponents should have the flexibility to design and conduct activities tailored to each refuge's unique habitats and management objectives in consideration of operational needs of oil and gas project proponents. Specifically, the new rule could help address the following impacts of oil and gas development on refuge resources.

- *Leaks and spills of oil, brine, or other contaminants.* Human health and safety can be compromised without adequate safeguards. In addition, soils, vegetation, water quality, fish and wildlife, and air quality can all be harmed by the release of contaminants.
- *Alteration of Fish and Wildlife Habitat.* Habitat can be altered, fragmented, or eliminated through oil and gas activities. These activities can also disturb and displace wildlife, cause physiological stress, and even result in wildlife deaths.
- *Introduction of invasive species.* The introduction of invasive species, especially along road and pipeline routes, can alter habitat. Disturbance caused by oil and gas activities can result in fundamental changes in ecological functions and processes, and lead to increased predation of declining species, reduced reproduction, and increased susceptibility to disease.
- *Adverse impact to public access and use.* Public uses of refuge areas may be restricted or prohibited by oil and gas operations. Although the areal extent of oil and gas exploration and production may be limited, the cumulative effects may extend to a much larger area.
- *Costs to taxpayers.* Poorly maintained sites or abandoned wells and infrastructure can place a burden on taxpayers as the cost of cleanup is borne by the Federal Government. In many cases, wells and infrastructure are abandoned due to inadequate finances by an operator. Having financial assurance to properly reclaim a site can save taxpayers from bearing the entire expense.

State oil and gas regulatory programs provide some level of Refuge System resource protection, but fundamentally have different roles and responsibilities. The Service is focused on meeting its legal mandate without duplicating State oversight. Our goal is to complement State regulatory programs to the benefit of the surface estate and the resources with which we are entrusted.

The Service has made progress in other areas to better address the complex challenge. We have formalized a Refuge System Energy Program and charged it with providing coordination and guidance to the Service leadership in promulgating the oil and gas regulations. Two major components of this coordination and guidance include: (1) improving consistency in oil and gas management; and (2) engaging Service staff, other Federal agencies and the public in revising regulations. Also, the Energy Program collaboratively develops and implements communication strategies to convey accurate information to a broad range of audiences and to engage the public and governmental entities in the rulemaking process.

The Service has hired three regional and three national oil and gas experts, including an environmental contaminants specialist and a petroleum engineer to support this effort. They provide assistance to Refuge System field staff and help develop national guidance and training. Other ways the Service is addressing this issue is the development of a national database of oil and gas wells and other structures on refuges. We have implemented annual oil and gas management training for nearly 200 Service staff. We are developing Service policy on management practices and have issued a Service handbook on management of oil and gas on refuges. These actions all contribute toward the core mission of the Service.

CONCLUSION

The Service's mission is working with others to conserve, protect, and enhance fish, wildlife, plants, and their habitats for the continuing benefit of the American people. A strong and effective oil and gas management program for the Refuge System that respects private property rights is essential to avoid unnecessary impacts that undermine the Service's ability to meet its statutory mandates and its mission. We have made strides in this area. Promulgation of revised regulations could help solidify progress that the Service has already made, and advance protection of trust resources for decades to come.

We believe rulemaking could support the Service in creating a consistent and reasonable set of regulatory management controls for non-Federal oil and gas activities occurring on refuges to both protect the public's surface interests while also providing reliable processes for industry.

We look forward to working with the subcommittee, as well as stakeholders, as we continue the process of considering rulemaking.

Dr. FLEMING. Thank you, Mr. Guertin. I can always tell when we have members from the Services because their timing is so perfect for 5 minutes. I mean you guys come within 15 seconds. It is amazing, how you do it. I guess it is the frequency that we have you up here. But we thank you for that.

Our next panelist—I may have mispronounced your name. I guess the K is not silent. So it is Knudson. Is that correct, sir?

Mr. KNUDSON. Yes, Mr. Chairman, that is correct.

Dr. FLEMING. OK, thank you. Well, I would like to now recognize you on behalf of the State of Alaska to present your testimony. And I yield to you.

STATEMENT OF KIP KNUDSON, DIRECTOR OF STATE AND FEDERAL RELATIONS, STATE OF ALASKA

Mr. KNUDSON. Chairman Fleming, Ranking Member Sablan, members of the committee, thank you for your time today. On behalf of Governor Parnell, I will just add some color comments to my written testimony, because a lot of very smart people helped me write that, and that is much better than, probably, what I will say today. Happy to try to answer questions, as well. My name is Kip Knudson. I am Governor Parnell's State Federal Director. I am located here, in Washington, DC.

As I am sure you have heard from Congressman Young a few times, Alaska is unique, under the law and in circumstance. It is a State of superlatives. Eighteen percent of the State's land is composed of refuges managed by a colleague here. That is 76.9 million acres of refuge lands in the State of Alaska.

I will spend a little bit of time today talking about the Kenai National Wildlife Refuge. This is a relatively large refuge, 1.9 million acres. As a point of comparison, Delaware is 1.6 million acres. Kenai is the tenth largest refuge in the United States. It is currently the only refuge that is experiencing oil and gas production in the State of Alaska.

So, besides all of the superlatives, Alaska is a world-renowned oil province. And yet, a very large percentage of our population struggles to have access to affordable energy. So, the ability to continue to look for and develop energy deposits that may be found underneath refuge lands is a very important concept in the State of Alaska.

So, let me just emphasize. In the written testimony we are asking very definitively for the U.S. Fish and Wildlife Service to treat Alaska as their sister Interior agencies have, and exempt Alaska from this rulemaking, if they persist. The two laws, National Interest Lands Conservation Act and the Native Claims Settlement Act, adequately govern all activity on refuge lands in the State of Alaska. There is no further need for additional regulation.

But for the rest of the United States, let me make a few observations—I am certainly not an expert. But if the goal of the rule or these rules pondered is to improve oil and gas activity, I am going to predict failure. And if the goal of the rules is to slow oil and gas activity, I am going to predict near-perfect success.

And let me—I learned quite a bit in this process. So, Interior governs oil and gas activity in a variety of ways. BLM is the primary manager for oil and gas activities on refuge lands where surface and subsurface are owned by the Federal Government, and where Native Americans, Indians, have subsurface rights. So BLM is the managing agency.

The proposal by U.S. Fish and Wildlife is really specific and very narrow. It is for non-Indian, split-estate oil and gas potential.

And then, finally, what is universal throughout the country is the States regulate almost all activity on all of these refuge lands, as well. And I will maintain today that the State is probably the expert regulator on all facets in all States. And I would like to emphasize as a second point that the Fish and Wildlife Service should save their time and effort, and spend more time coordinating and cooperating with the State regulators to see how they can crack this nut in a much more efficient way.

So, the origin of the rulemaking is referenced to GAO reports. I have a peer petition here from 2011. But a lot of it is focusing on the sins of the past on refuge lands. And I want to urge members of the committee to not focus necessarily on the sins of the past, because activity that occurred 40, 50, 60 years ago clearly was occurring in the Dark Ages. Industry activity these days is a totally different kettle of fish.

Back to that GAO report, there has been a more recent one, specifically working with BLM's management and oversight of oil and gas activities. And most of the bullets—in fact, all of the bullets—really target ensuring that the BLM is working most efficiently, not creating new rules and regimes and adding more staff to regulate oil and gas activity. So I want to emphasize that they—even the GAO emphasized that the BLM should go and work with the States, specifically.

And then, finally, we find a little bit of irony in this topic, because the only problem we have with oil and gas and operators in the State of Alaska is one operator, and that is the Federal Government. We have sites all over the State of Alaska, where oil and gas activity has turned out to be a disaster.

This is from the Umiat Field in northern Alaska. This was taken when the activity was going on. I think Corps of Engineers was working this. This massive stuff here, these are all barrels full of God knows what. They were just buried and left. And the Department of the Interior still today is on the hook for many hundreds of millions of dollars of environmental degradation. We would urge that the Department of the Interior focus on cleaning up these messes first, and let the States worry about the private oil and gas activity.

Thank you, Mr. Chairman.

[The prepared statement of Mr. Knudson follows:]

PREPARED STATEMENT OF KIP C. KNUDSON, DIRECTOR OF STATE/FEDERAL RELATIONS, OFFICE OF GOVERNOR SEAN PARNELL, STATE OF ALASKA

I. INTRODUCTION

Chairman Fleming, Ranking Member Sablan, and members of the House Subcommittee on Fisheries, Wildlife, Oceans and Insular Affairs—for the record I am Kip C. Knudson, Director of State/Federal Relations for the State of Alaska (the State). On behalf of Governor Sean Parnell, I thank the subcommittee for this opportunity to testify and express our support for your work to ensure that the natural values of our National Wildlife Refuges continue to be preserved for the public benefit while allowing for the responsible development of natural resources within their boundaries consistent with law. We appreciate your leadership in striking and maintaining this balance.

In particular, I thank you for the opportunity to bring to your attention the unique aspects—and successes—of oil and gas development in the National Wildlife Refuges in Alaska. In addition to the National Wildlife Refuge System Administration Act [1] and other broadly applicable laws, we have a unique framework of existing Federal law—primarily the Alaska Native Claims Settlement Act of 1971 (ANCSA) [2] and the Alaska National Interest Lands Conservation Act of 1980 (ANILCA) [3]—which provide for the management of oil and gas activity within refuges and maintain a workable balance in Alaska's unique environment.

The State's interests in this activity are significant. For example, oil and gas exploration and development occurring today in the KNWR is essential for providing natural gas to heat and power the homes and businesses in much of the southcentral region of Alaska, including the major population centers of Anchorage, the Kenai Peninsula, and the Matanuska-Susitna Valley. Oil from these fields is also refined in Alaska to meet motor-vehicle demand throughout the State. We welcome Congress's oversight of the proposed U.S. Fish and Wildlife Service (USFWS) rulemaking—which may affect the livelihoods and energy security of many Alaskans.

Overview of Today's Testimony

My primary message is that there is a robust framework of existing State and Federal law that rigorously regulates oil and gas development within the boundaries of the National Wildlife Refuges in Alaska. This framework is unique to Alaska and was specifically tailored by Congress to provide for the national interest and the economic and social needs of Alaskans. A cohesive and long-standing suite of Alaska laws, regulations and policies have been developed consistent with this framework and have proven, in practice, to be a testament to Congress' foresight. For this reason, the USFWS should provide, at a minimum, a categorical exemption from the proposed rulemaking for the Refuges located in Alaska.

Any changes to national-level USFWS regulations must not, and under law cannot, avoid very explicitly acknowledging the balance Congress has already struck in Alaska, and should not upset or duplicate it. While the refuge lands in Alaska contain a huge portion—approximately 50 percent—of the National Wildlife Refuge System's total acreage, Alaska is home to only 16 of the over 550 National Wildlife Refuges throughout the country. In this context, it could be said the USFWS administers 2 sets of Refuge lands—the 16 expansive Alaska Refuges and the other, much smaller 535 refuges. The most efficient way to acknowledge and respect Alaska's unique circumstances and functioning management structure in the context of the current proposed regulations is for the USFWS to include an unambiguous and categorical exemption for the 16 Alaska refuges.

As I will detail below, Congress has already spoken on this issue in 1980 by providing clear instructions to the USFWS for managing Alaska's Refuge network under ANILCA and ANCSA. Ethan Schutt, Executive Vice President of Cook Inlet Region, Incorporated will speak in much greater detail on ANCSA and how it guides the Federal management of oil and gas activities in Alaska refuges. The State appreciates Congressional oversight to ensure that the USFWS understands and adheres to the spirit and letter of these existing laws.

I also want to again emphasize the importance of continuing oil and gas exploration and development within Alaskan Refuges to the Americans who reside in Alaska. Gas produced in the Cook Inlet area, including gas from fields within the Kenai National Wildlife Refuge (KNWR), is the primary source of both heat and electricity for over half the State's population, and the reserves in the Cook Inlet area provide for the energy security critical to sustaining our livelihoods into the future. Without these stable local supplies and reserves, the high costs of living that Alaskans face would be dramatically exacerbated.

Please note that the State has already submitted formal comments to the USFWS on the topic we are discussing today pursuant to the Federal Register Advanced Notice of Proposed Rulemaking (ANPR). These comments are consistent with the testimony I am providing and are attached to my written testimony, for the record.

---

[1] 16 U.S.C. §§ 668dd–668ee.
[2] 43 U.S.C. §§ 1601 et. seq.
[3] 16 U.S.C. §§ 3101 et. seq.

II. THE UNPARALLELED SIZE AND SCOPE OF NATIONAL WILDLIFE REFUGES WITHIN ALASKA

Alaska contains an extensive network of Federal land ownership—approximately 222 of the 640 million acres owned by the Federal Government are located in Alaska. Of these 222 million acres of Federal land, roughly 75 million are in the 16 National Wildlife Refuges distributed throughout the State. This is 75 of the 150 million total acres managed by the USFWS nationwide—roughly 50 percent of the National Wildlife Refuge System. Alaska includes 14 of the 15 largest wildlife refuges in the country, nine of which contain more than two million acres each. Alaska's smallest wildlife refuge, the Izembek National Wildlife Refuge, is almost half the size of the State of Rhode Island.

In sheer magnitude alone, Alaska's Refuge lands are in a distinct category within the Refuge System. Coupled with the unique land ownership issues associated with Alaska's Statehood entitlement and Alaska Native Corporation (ANC) entitlements under ANCSA, which I will discuss below, Alaska requires a customized approach to refuge management. Fortunately, Congress did exactly that through these two pieces of legislation that direct the management of Federal lands and protect private rights in Alaska's network of refuges.

III. A BRIEF HISTORY OF ALASKA'S UNIQUE LAND OWNERSHIP PATTERNS AND LEGAL REGIMES APPLICABLE TO REFUGES

The Federal policy of retaining land in Federal ownership began in the early 1900s. This resulted in large swaths of public lands being created and maintained in the western States, as I'm sure some of the subcommittee members can readily attest to. This policy was well established when Alaska became a State in 1959, but there was still much that was not known about Alaska's varied and abundant natural resources.

When Alaska entered the union, it was apparent that learning more about, and utilizing these natural resources would be critical to the massive State's economic future, from its abundant fish and game to its mineral and geologic potential. During the transition from territory to State, Congress agreed that a portion of the State— approximately 105 million of 365 million acres—would be transferred to the new State government for management and development under the terms of the Statehood Compact.

However, very serious land management issues were left unresolved by the Compact. First and foremost, Alaska Natives, who had lived in Alaska for thousands of years and, many of whom practiced a subsistence lifestyle, had important but unaddressed claims to lands. In 1971, Congress, recognizing the need for resolution of these issues, passed ANCSA.

The central result of ANCSA was the creation and capitalization of 12 ANCs. Under the act, Alaska Natives enrolled as shareholders in their respective ANC, and also in smaller Village Corporations representing the communities comprising the larger regional areas. A central part of the act allowed each ANC to own land, generally within its region and surrounding communities, via selection and conveyance. When the conveyance process is completed, the total land entitlement to be transferred to ANCs under these provisions will be approximately 44 million acres. ANCSA provided for the ownership of surface rights, subsurface rights, or both in different scenarios, resulting in areas of split estate ownership throughout the State. ANCs have rights and, in fact, an obligation to develop these lands for the benefit of their shareholders.

To accommodate the negotiations and ultimate resolution of ANCSA, the State's land selection activity was effectively paused during most of the 1960s and early 1970s. At this time, as more people came to Alaska and saw its natural beauty, and as the State's young economy was growing, there was a push to conserve more Federal lands in Alaska.

Alaskans and Congress viewed ANILCA as the "grand compromise"—to achieve "proper balance" [4] between the use and conservation of Federal land in Alaska. Under the legislation, over 148 million acres of Federal lands were placed into Conservation System Units (CSUs). The CSUs, around 60 percent of the lands in Federal ownership, were placed off-limits to the State and ANCs for further selection, while also limiting the possibility of future economic development of these lands by Alaskans.

ANILCA created, expanded, and consolidated Alaskan Refuges to establish the current network of 16 refuges, which collectively comprise over 20 percent of the

---

[4] See 16 U.S.C. § 3101(d).

14

State. This enormous expansion of the refuge system resulted in considerable State and ANC acreage (both surface and subsurface) suddenly located within or effectively surrounded by a CSU.

This distinctive history has resulted in a very unique and diverse land ownership pattern in Alaska, with enormous amounts of land in Federal CSUs, less than 1 percent in individual private ownership, as well as scattered State and ANC selections and land holdings throughout the State.

ANILCA also provided Alaska with an exclusive framework of controlling Federal law. In exchange for setting aside such a substantial percentage of the State in CSUs, ANILCA's "compromise" included numerous provisions to protect Alaskans' interests in access to the State's natural resources, especially those needed for the developing economy and infrastructure. ANCSA and ANILCA contain numerous provisions that promote and guide access to and utilization of Alaska's natural resources, including those resources surrounded by Alaska Refuges.

Most of these provisions explicitly control activity in Alaska notwithstanding any other law. For example, the Refuge System Improvement Act of 1997[5] includes a specific savings clause to ensure that, in the event of a conflict between any provision of the Act and any provision of ANILCA, the provisions of ANILCA prevail. Because these Federal laws only affect Alaska, national policymakers and regulators do not always understand this important point when first approaching Alaska issues. To raise awareness of this framework and to enforce these legal rights, State experts frequently remind Federal officials about the statutory directives to consult with the State on issues affecting CSUs such as Alaska's refuges.

IV. THE COMPELLING PUBLIC INTEREST IN ROBUST PRODUCTION IN COOK INLET—INCLUDING THE KNWR

Although not the only refuge with significant oil and gas potential, the only refuge with oil and gas production in Alaska today[6] is the KNWR, arguably one of the refuge system's most beautiful and frequently visited. It includes almost two million acres east and south of Cook Inlet on the Kenai Peninsula, with its northern boundary a mere 10 air-miles south of Anchorage across the Cook Inlet. The refuge's history stretches back to the Kenai National Moose Range created in 1941 by President Franklin D. Roosevelt.

The entire Cook Inlet area features significant oil and gas potential, and many identified formations are located under the boundaries of the Refuge. The land within the Refuge has seen oil and gas activity for nearly 60 years, beginning with the development of Cook Inlet's first field, Swanson River, in 1956 and 1957. Some have said it was this major oil find that tipped the national balance in favor of accepting Alaska as the 49th State in 1959. Production in Swanson River continues today and is a critical piece of the energy supply for the most populous region of Alaska.

When Alaska's oil and gas production is discussed, many people naturally think of the North Slope oil fields. As some of the largest in the western hemisphere, these fields, including the mammoth fields of Prudhoe Bay and Kuparuk, have produced over 16 billion barrels of crude oil to date. The Trans-Alaska Pipeline System, one of the Nation's most impressive infrastructure projects, transports this Arctic oil from the North Slope to Gulf of Alaska tidewater in Valdez and is the backbone of our State's resource economy. But it is Alaska's original oil discoveries in southcentral Alaska, and the access to the region's abundant natural gas resources that oil production made possible, which continue to be the most important source of domestic energy supplies for a majority of Alaskans.

Extensive oil and gas exploration followed the development of Swanson River in the 1960s, and activity quickly moved to the east and west sides of Cook Inlet as well as off-shore. The natural gas supplies that have been produced from these areas have long been used to generate electricity and provide heat for Alaskans living in the southcentral region. Today, a majority of Alaska's population is located in this area—due in part to the stable cost of energy Cook Inlet has provided for half of a century. Cook Inlet natural gas has also been used for industrial purposes to support Alaska's economy, as well as for pioneering liquefied natural gas (LNG) exports from the United States' oldest, and for decades, only LNG export facility in Nikiski, Alaska. To date, approximately 11 trillion cubic feet of natural gas have been produced from the Inlet.

Cook Inlet producers continue to provide natural gas to meet southcentral Alaska's demand for approximately 80 to 90 billion cubic feet per year. Thanks to

[5]P.L. 105–57, amending 16 U.S.C. §668dd.
[6]There are three producing Federal units—Swanson River, Beaver Creek, and Birch Hill—that are within the refuge boundaries.

its significant untapped resource potential and the competitive investment climate fostered by Governor Parnell and the Alaska Legislature, the basin, after over 50 years of sustained activity, is now even experiencing a welcome boom. We call it the Cook Inlet Renaissance. Motivated companies are moving into the Inlet to explore new fields and revitalize existing ones, and residents are benefiting from new reserves being brought online. This includes work-overs in the Federal lease areas operating within the KNWR that are facilitated by the extensive existing oil and gas delivery infrastructure which partially lies within the Refuge's boundaries. Industry has also been engaged in USFWS-permitted resource exploration of private lands within Refuge boundaries, which will hopefully contribute to future Cook Inlet production and additional energy security for Alaskans.

While we strongly believe Cook Inlet's available supplies are adequate to meet demand in the near term, it is important to understand the compelling State interest in ensuring robust production from all the resource-rich lands, including Refuge lands, in Cook Inlet. In the past when some entities predicted a downturn in Cook Inlet activity, one of primary proposals to meet the southcentral region's energy needs involved foreign LNG imports. The energy supplies that come from Cook Inlet, including natural gas being supplied from lands within and adjacent to the Kenai Refuge, cannot be immediately replaced if burdened or impeded by excessive regulation.

Pursuant to ANCSA and ANILCA, non-Federal surface and subsurface estates also are to be found within the boundaries of other refuges in Alaska. These estates tend to be located in regions of the State where energy costs are orders of magnitude higher than those in southcentral Alaska. It is imperative that the State and Federal Government work in the smartest, most responsible manner to ensure that those resource-rich lands are not effectively put off limits due to poorly crafted regulation. To sustain the Cook Inlet renaissance, and to allow a similar renaissance to occur in other regions by attracting diligent, responsible companies eager to deploy state-of-the-art, low-impact technologies, Alaska needs to ensure consistent application of rights in ANILCA and ANCSA that support this activity. Federal and State managers, as well as industry leaders, already work within this specifically tailored framework to make responsible decisions regarding Alaska's unique environment.

V. THE ROLE OF FEDERAL OIL AND GAS DEVELOPMENT WITHIN NATIONAL WILDLIFE REFUGES TO ALASKA

Before continuing with the substance of my testimony, I would like to make a brief note about the scope of the proposed rulemaking under review by the subcommittee today.

As the State understands the USFWS's February 24th Advanced Notice of Proposed Rulemaking (ANPR), the USFWS is gathering information related to non-Federal oil and gas development within the boundaries of our National Wildlife Refuge System. The ANPR describes such development as including—''those activities associated with any private, State, or tribally owned mineral interest where the surface estate is administered by the Service as part of the Refuge system.'' The State interprets this to mean the regulations would not impact Federal oil and gas activities within the Refuge System. There are currently three producing leases within the Kenai Refuge on Federal surface and subsurface estate—Beaver Creek, Swanson River, and Birch Hill—that would be considered Federal oil and gas developments. These fields are critical to providing natural gas supplies to many Alaskans, as discussed above.

This would mean that the regulations would not change Federal oil and gas development, but instead would affect activity related to non-Federal surface and subsurface estates and potentially destabilize the careful balance of ANCSA and ANILCA described above.

VI. THE NEED FOR A CATEGORICAL EXEMPTION FOR ALASKA FROM THE NEW RULEMAKING REGARDING NON-FEDERAL OIL AND GAS DEVELOPMENT

Turning to those activities the State understands to be the subject of the ANPR, there are four points that I would like to make today that support the USFWS including a categorical exemption for the 16 Alaska Refuges from the potential rulemaking.

The ANPR contemplates adding an unnecessary layer of regulation.

First, the USFWS has Alaska-specific oil and gas rules in place, so adding a new layer has the potential create confusion and delay. Additionally, new rules will necessarily further distract USFWS from executing on the core missions for which regulations are already in place.

The State currently has in place regulatory systems that govern aspects of oil and gas activity from exploration through dismantlement, repair and restoration. Most of this regulation is enforced on an operator regardless of the land status on which the activity occurs. The State prioritizes this regulatory authority, ensures that is funded, and regularly verifies that it is keeping pace with technology and ever-improving environmental practices.

This regulatory expertise, when added to the Alaska-specific laws and rules, guarantees that no certainty will be gained in Alaska. Additionally, the refuge system will be no more protected while the taxpayer will see limited refuge resources squandered. Effectively, USFWS will have misapplied resources at the expense of missions only that agency executes.

A perfect example is the current back-log of Endangered Species Act work USFWS is experiencing. This back-log is currently having a negative impact on the species the ESA intends to protect and has delayed and hampered economic opportunity for Alaskans. The threat of uninformed Section 7 consultations resulting in ''preferred alternatives'' to remove ''Jeopardy'' and ''Adverse Modifications'' findings has had a chilling effect on resource development investments in Alaska. For reference, the extent of these significant impacts is described in the State's study of potential impacts from the unnecessary listing of polar bear.

The ANPR demonstrates inconsistency with Alaskan land ownership patterns.

The ANPR outlines that the USFWS's scoping effort will address the perceived lack of a cohesive and sufficiently detailed authorization framework for non-Federal oil and gas activities within Refuges. More specifically, the USFWS would like to develop a homogenous means of managing ''those activities associated with any private, State, or tribally owned mineral interest where the surface estate is administered by the Service as part of the Refuge system.''

The current regulation used for this purpose similarly focuses on Federal lands overlying private rights which were retained upon the area's conveyance to or acquisition by the government.[7] As discussed above, there are areas in Alaska with ''inholdings'' within a refuge, where an entity, often an ANC, owns both the surface and the subsurface or mineral estate, of a parcel. In these scenarios, the surface land may be administered as part of the refuge but it is held as the property of the ANC. These properties have special rights of access and utilization under ANCSA and ANILCA that would be very different than the scenarios apparently contemplated by the USFWS where a third party owns some portion or reserved right of the subsurface estate. Understandably the language of the ANPR is phrased generally, but this is a threshold example of why an Alaska exemption will provide the most clarity for both the USFWS and the regulated public. Trying to fit Alaska into this rulemaking effort would introduce the need for the USFWS to conduct extensive research and analysis to understand all of Alaska's unique land ownership scenarios, complicating rather than adding clarity to the rulemaking.

The ANPR addresses issues that are not pertinent to Alaska Refuges due to the Alaska-specific authorization process based in existing Federal law.

My testimony so far has repeated the fact that ANCSA and ANILCA gave Alaskans and ANCs a suite of access rights to and utilization of lands within the State, including in-holdings within the boundaries of Alaska Refuges. This includes rights to support economic development of property interests and to establish infrastructure to further these interests.[8] Any regulations the USFWS promulgates regarding non-Federal oil and gas development that do apply to Alaska will have to comply with these statutes and valid existing rights.

As the USFWS has stated in the ANPR, one goal of the proposed rulemaking is to eliminate an ''uncertain and inconsistent'' regulatory environment for oil and gas operators in National Wildlife Refuges.[9] To apply to Alaska Refuges under the existing Federal law, a nationally applicable rule would require extensive cross-references, exemptions, disclaimers and qualifying statements. This would hardly support clarity or consistency for the regulated public. A clearer approach, which provides a much more effective use of the USFWS's rule-writing time and resources, would be to include a categorical exemption for Alaska which clarifies that any new regulation of non-Federal oil and gas activities does not apply to refuges in Alaska.

---

[7] See 50 CFR § 29.32.
[8] See, *e.g.*, ANILCA § 1101 for the approval of transportation and utility projects, ANILCA § 1109 for all valid rights of access pre-dating ANILCA's enactment, ANILCA § 1110(b) for the economic use of subsurface rights, ANILCA § 1111(a) for the right of temporary access across Federal lands related to non-federally owned lands, etc.
[9] 79 Fed. Reg. 10080, 10081.

It is important to point out that Alaska Refuges have already developed and implemented procedures and standards for the authorization of non-Federal oil and gas activities consistent with ANILCA and ANCSA. For example, the USFWS recently issued complex authorizations for high-tech, low-impact seismic activities within the KNWR that will occur over several of the next exploration seasons. Historically, there has also been production from non-Federal oil and gas areas. This is in addition to the long-standing Federal oil and gas development activities that are in production today that show oil and gas operations can be compatible with Refuge lands that are mentioned above. The evaluation and approval mechanisms the USFWS and Kenai Refuge staff have employed with Alaska's unique legal framework to provide flexibility and maintain consistent expectations for property owners, regulated entities, and the public should not be confused by this national rulemaking.

The ANPR references corollary National Park Service regulations that contain a categorical exemption for Alaska.

Throughout the ANPR, the USFWS asks commenters to consider possible models for the scope and content of the proposed rule. In particular, the ANPR includes a discrete section asking whether National Park Service (NPS) regulations regarding the management of similar activities in National Parks should be used as a model for the USFWS regulations under consideration. In the referenced regulations,[10] the NPS explicitly recognized the role ANILCA plays in managing these activities in Alaska and, for many of the reasons I have noted in my testimony, included a categorical exemption for Alaska parklands from the national regulations.

In this respect, the State finds the NPS regulation provides an ideal model for the proposed rule and requests that it also include such an Alaska-specific categorical exemption.

VII. CONCLUSION

Consistent with the comments already submitted pursuant to the administrative process, the State strongly believes that the most efficient and effective path forward for the USFWS is to include at a minimum a categorical exemption for Alaskan Refuges due to the complexities of ANILCA and ANCSA. As discussed above, the NPS has taken this approach so that they can move forward with developing regulatory models for the other jurisdictions that are not part of Alaska's unique legal framework.

I also hope that the general narrative information I provided is helpful to the subcommittee for framing this issue. It has been my purpose to show that the unique legal regimes that control Federal activity in Alaska today grew out of Alaska's unique history and environment, including its immense resource potential, unparalleled conservation, and absolute size. When Congress originally enacted these laws, it was striking a very careful balance that intended to carve out Alaskans' rights and Federal protections.

Finally, I wish to repeat how critical continued oil and gas development in Alaska's National Wildlife Refuges can be—to our citizens' electricity and heat in addition to economic livelihood. This is clearly demonstrated in the KNWR, where over 50 years of oil and gas activity has provided energy supplies for many of the Alaskans in the State. This development serves as an example of both the potential and importance of developing oil and gas in a compatible fashion with National Wildlife Refuges. While I cannot speak to instances in other States, I suspect the long-term success of the Kenai Wildlife Refuge could be found elsewhere.

––––––

Dr. FLEMING. Thank you, Mr. Knudson. Thank you for your testimony, and Mr. Guertin, as well.

At this point we would have some questions from the dais to our panel members. And I now recognize myself for 5 minutes.

Mr. Guertin, there are about 100 national wildlife refuges that have actively producing oil and gas wells. When the Fish and Wildlife Service acquired the land, did your realty office know there were non-Federal minerals, and that your agency was not purchasing those subsurface rights?

––––––

[10] See 36 CFR § 13.15(d)(2).

Mr. GUERTIN. Mr. Chairman, the way the Service operates is to acquire the least amount of interest in any type of property as we move forward, in order for us to accomplish our mission. In many cases, the United States has only purchased the surface estate, and has not purchased the corollary subsurface estate. So we had no idea, nor did we do evaluation as to whether or not there were minerals underneath that at that time.

Dr. FLEMING. But you were aware that there were actively producing oil and gas wells, or certainly well could be.

Mr. GUERTIN. There could have been. Yes——

Dr. FLEMING. You really weren't asking the question, either way. Your realty office was purchasing the land, or acquiring the land in some way, regardless of whether there were oil and gas wells, or minerals—under the surface.

Mr. GUERTIN. Yes, Mr. Chairman, for the pre-eminent wildlife values on that land.

Dr. FLEMING. Right. So you purchased these lands with your eyes open, so to speak, or at least capable of having your eyes open, whether you chose to look for any well activity or not. There was no one who forced the Service to acquire this property. You weren't required by anyone else to buy the property, regardless of whether there was activity on it or not.

Mr. GUERTIN. No, Mr. Chairman.

Dr. FLEMING. Thank you. Can the Fish and Wildlife Service deny access to subsurface minerals that it does not own?

Mr. GUERTIN. Mr. Chairman, the Service recognizes and respects that this is private property, and we cannot deny access to it. We can, however, work with the owners to get into there in a reasonable and prudent way to avoid significant impacts to the wildlife values of the refuge around it.

Dr. FLEMING. I am not sure if I caught all of that. You said that you can't——

Mr. GUERTIN. We cannot——

Dr. FLEMING [continuing]. Deny access. And what was the other part?

Mr. GUERTIN. We cannot deny them access, Mr. Chairman, but we can work with them to avoid and mitigate any of the impacts of their ongoing development to the larger wildlife refuge, and in partnership with them.

Dr. FLEMING. If you did deny access, that would be a violation of the Fifth Amendment, the Constitution?

Mr. GUERTIN. Yes, Mr. Chairman. We agree with that.

Dr. FLEMING. OK, thank you. If I am drilling a well from my own property and, through the use of horizontal drilling, extracting oil and gas resources which I own from underneath a wildlife refuge, is the Service currently regulating those activities? That is I am drilling in private land, but I am horizontally moving underneath the refuge for the mineral rights that I may own.

Mr. GUERTIN. There have been——

Dr. FLEMING. Is the Service currently regulating those activities?

Mr. GUERTIN. We are working on some projects with that. In fact, it is taking place, Mr. Chairman. What we are envisioning for the future is, as technologies emerge, there is going to be a lot more of that going on. And we are also addressing things at a larger landscape scale, where private lands and the refuge itself are pretty closely inter-related.

Dr. FLEMING. But as it stands, you are not regulating that activity. You are contemplating some sort of future regulation.

Mr. GUERTIN. Yes, Mr. Chairman.

Dr. FLEMING. OK. What are your intentions as to those activities in the future? And I guess maybe you have already answered, and that is you are reviewing that and still in the process of deciding how you may do that in the future.

Mr. GUERTIN. Yes, Mr. Chairman. What we have done is move forward and put out for public review and comment an advanced notice of proposed rulemaking, which, in essence, is asking a series of questions to all of the stakeholders—the industry, States, Tribes, and private land owners—as we move forward.

What we envision over the next 2 years is working through a public process to solicit ideas, information, and come up with a framework——

Dr. FLEMING. All right. But let me ask you this. Do you contemplate treating those that are, again, drilled on private land but underneath refuge land any differently than those that are actively drilling on the refuge land?

Mr. GUERTIN. Yes, Mr. Chairman. We are envisioning—probably looking at a larger landscape approach, which might include some of this adjacent land. We have not made a final determination as to that. But we are certainly going to evaluate this during the process. But open to all the feedback we get on that point.

Dr. FLEMING. OK, thank you. Mr. Guertin, the State of Alaska has testified that they inspect the 80 oil and gas wells at the Kenai—I guess I am saying that correctly—Kenai National Wildlife Refuge at least twice a year. Is that a sufficient number, or is there something unique about the Federal Government that requires further inspections?

Mr. GUERTIN. Do you mean the State is inspecting them for health and safety at this point, Mr. Chairman.

Dr. FLEMING. Well, the State is inspecting them twice a year. Is that inadequate?

Mr. GUERTIN. Well, a lot of the State regulatory framework is really dealing with the machinery and the down-hole functioning of the wells. It is dealing with a lot of the production values. We don't have any regulatory authority currently to inspect any of these wells at this point in time. What we do is evaluate potential impacts that come off of these wells.

Dr. FLEMING. But you do contemplate possibly beginning to regulate that. So again, the question is, if they are already regulating in Alaska and in Louisiana, is there a need for a whole other layer of regulation?

Mr. GUERTIN. There may not be. If the best practices that States employ are going to support our mission, we would certainly look at that through this rulemaking process, Mr. Chairman. We could very well adopt State standards. If they are not up to what we need to manage the Refuge System, we will evaluate that during this rulemaking process.

Dr. FLEMING. OK. My time is up, and I yield to the Ranking Member for 5 minutes.

Mr. SABLAN. Thank you very much, Mr. Chairman. Mr. Guertin—is that——

Mr. GUERTIN. Mr. Guertin, sir.

Mr. SABLAN. Mr. Guertin. The 2003 GAO report recommended that the Service clarify its permitting authority of non-Federal O&G operations through regulations. Would updated regulations provide a more consistent and reasonable set of rules over all oil and gas activities occurring on the Refuge System to protect the public's surface interests?

Mr. GUERTIN. Our vision is that having a consistent framework for the entire National Wildlife Refuge System would make it easier for our refuge managers to focus on their mission of safeguarding the public's investment in the National Wildlife Refuge System. At the same time, it would give operators a consistent series of larger, strategic guidelines they could tier off of.

We are also envisioning that we would step down these at the local level, much as we do our CCP process, to give the refuge managers the opportunity to work with operators at a local scale, as well. But we——

Mr. SABLAN. So——

Mr. GUERTIN [continuing]. Believe the framework is necessary to set that kind of standard for the national system, as a whole.

Mr. SABLAN. So there is—because right now I think there is—different States have different ways to regulate this, and it is just—you know.

But—so let me ask you another question, Mr. Guertin. How do people get onto a wildlife refuge to access fossil fuels?

Mr. GUERTIN. Essentially, there is no formal process at this point, sir. If operators have legal rights to the property, their minerals underneath the surface estate there, they have the prerogative to just come onto the refuge. Oftentimes we might find out after the fact.

What we are envisioning is, instead, partnering with them at the beginning of a process, and working with them to avoid and minimize any potential unintended impacts that this development might incur.

Mr. SABLAN. And——

Mr. GUERTIN. Right now there is no framework to——

Mr. SABLAN. And so——

Mr. GUERTIN [continuing]. Have them go through a process.

Mr. SABLAN. So does this unfettered and unregulated access cause damage to wildlife and habitat, or any other problem?

Mr. GUERTIN. Well, there has been some anecdotal evidence of operators going down to a refuge without our knowing about it. But most of the impacts have been from older wells that—the caps have failed on them, or there have been leaks over time, or the breakdown in machinery, sir.

Mr. SABLAN. Yes. And some in Congress always complain about the refuge system maintenance backlog. So can you please tell us—talk about potential future damages from abandoned oil and gas wells on refuge lands?

Mr. GUERTIN. Well, there have been some cases where we have experienced oil leaks or saline water leaks. There has been damage from equipment to the Refuge System. There has been damage to roads. Seepage or drainage has gotten into wetlands and estuarian areas. And so what we are envisioning is partnering with the industry, moving forward in a proactive way, to help them plan and evaluate where to site the equipment they will need to operate in the future and avoid any unnecessary environmental degradation in the years to come.

Mr. SABLAN. Let me go further out. And let me ask, because in your advanced notice of proposed rulemaking the Service says that the Refuge System has sustained significant damages to refuge resources from leaks and spills, inadequate plugging, abandonment, and reclamation.

And you are not going to be able to answer this question today, but I would like to ask you if you could supply the subcommittee with a more exact counting of the cost the taxpayers have to bear to fix the damage from these leaks and spills and other cleanup. When you say ''significant damage,'' can you put a dollar figure on that? And not just how much taxpayers had to pay in the past, but also how much future liability are we looking at. And maybe you can't provide that information now.

Mr. GUERTIN. We can provide information for the record. There have been some documented spills that have cost anywhere from $200,000 to up to $1.2 million for remediation on individual sites on the National Wildlife Refuge System——

Mr. SABLAN. All right.

Mr. GUERTIN [continuing]. Tied to oil damage.

Mr. SABLAN. So I am going to go back to my previous question, or the question before that, on the backlog. Let me ask you. How does removal of and liability for these structures contribute to the backlog? I am talking about the maintenance backlog and the abandoned oil and gas wells and refuge lands. How does the removal and liability contribute to the backlog?

Mr. GUERTIN. If the refuge has abandoned equipment and an unplugged well, old pads, settling ponds, or buildings, or rigs, they would be included in the refuge deferred maintenance backlog, and would be the taxpayers' responsibility to pay to remove or properly mitigate for those removal or damages. That would contribute to the backlog. Yes, sir.

Mr. SABLAN. Thank you very much. I yield back, Mr. Chairman.

Dr. FLEMING. The gentleman yields back. The Chair now recognizes Mr. Duncan of South Carolina.

Mr. DUNCAN. Thank you, Mr. Chairman. Thank you, gentlemen, for being here.

Mr. Guertin, what is the prioritization of the EIS, in relation to other priorities for the Fish and Wildlife Service?

Mr. GUERTIN. It is one of probably the top 10 or 15 priorities for the National Wildlife Refuge System management going forward, Mr. Congressman.

Mr. DUNCAN. OK. Under—well, let me ask you this. Under what statutory authority can the Service stipulate how a company may explore for its oil and gas resources within the Refuge System?

Mr. GUERTIN. Could you rephrase the question, sir?

Mr. DUNCAN. Yes sir. Under what statutory authority can the Service stipulate how a company may explore for its oil and gas resources within the Refuge System?

Mr. GUERTIN. Sure. We are citing a Refuge Organic Act, the Refuge Improvement Act of 1996, as our organic Act that gives us the authority to manage the Nation's National Wildlife Refuge System, with a responsibility to manage for conservation and wildlife first. That organic legislation also dictates that we provide CCPs, or Comprehensive Conservation Plans for each unit of the National Wildlife Refuge System that drive how we are going to manage the program, going forward.

We cannot stop any land owner from getting to their property minerals underneath the wildlife refuge system, but we believe this legislation gives us the authority to partner with them to help them develop and extract this resource with the least amount of impact to the larger refuge unit, itself.

Mr. DUNCAN. So let me just follow up. How would you respond to a GAO report in 2007 which cited, ''We believe it is for Congress, not the DOI, to weigh the needs of the refuge lands and interests of the mineral owners, and, ultimately, to determine what oversight authority would be appropriate''? How would you respond to that?

Mr. GUERTIN. Our agency and the Administration would point to the Refuge Organic Act, the National Wildlife Refuge System Improvement Act, as giving us that authority. Clearly, we are interested in working with Congress as we plumb this issue further in the coming months and years through this proposed rulemaking. And so that is how we would go about answering that question.

Mr. DUNCAN. OK. Just shift gears for a second. This is just fact-finding for me. Have there been any major oil spills from exploration or production within the Refuge System?

Mr. GUERTIN. We can provide for the record some specifics, but there have been no significant oil spills from exploration on the Refuge System. Most of them have been from——

Mr. DUNCAN. Are these pipeline spills? Are those the spills——

Mr. GUERTIN. Pipeline——

Mr. DUNCAN [continuing]. At the wellhead themselves?

Mr. GUERTIN. Yes, sir.

Mr. DUNCAN. Pipeline?

Mr. GUERTIN. Pipeline spills, or there has been some leakage off of some of the well pads and things like that.

Mr. DUNCAN. OK. So during the past 10 years, how many total barrels of oil would you guesstimate—you can provide me specifics later—from the oil wells within the Refuge System?

Mr. GUERTIN. I would have to provide that information for the record, Mr. Congressman.

Mr. DUNCAN. OK. If you could provide that, that would be great for the whole committee.

And, Mr. Chairman, I really don't have anything else. We will just wait on that information to come back from him.

Dr. FLEMING. The gentleman yields back. Mr. Lowenthal, do you have questions?

Dr. LOWENTHAL. Thank you, Mr. Chair. The question—Mr. Guertin, thank you for coming and testifying before the committee.

When I read the GAO report's recommendation to the Service, and then also the Service's advanced notice of proposed rulemaking, so it seems like the Service now is—as you pointed out, is finally addressing the problems that the GAO first uncovered in 2003 and again in 2007. Is that it? So——

Mr. GUERTIN. Yes, there has been a lot of unprecedented development going on in the country, there has been a lot of interest in moving forward on a lot of projects. There are a lot of emerging technologies. The time is very ripe for the Fish and Wildlife Service——

Dr. LOWENTHAL. Right.

Mr. GUERTIN [continuing]. To partner with industry and promulgate these regulations for certainty, moving forward.

Dr. LOWENTHAL. I think the point that I am also—and while you didn't mention it much in your oral testimony—in your written— that this is a real problem. It is not trying to create a problem. It has been documented by the GAO and—the two—I recall the two case studies in your prepared testimony also cost the taxpayers over $1.5 million. The public deserves, I think, a consistent and reasonable set of regulatory and management controls of oil and gas activities occurring on the Refuge System to protect the public's surface interests.

So, the first question I have is, do other Federal land management agencies manage split-estate lands?

Mr. GUERTIN. There are some instances in the National Park Service, in the National Forest System. Largely, the BLM would have dual estate ownership of this. Fish and Wildlife Service, again, has entered into some conservation practices by acquiring the least amount of title to a property we needed to deliver our mission. That has meant we probably have more of this split estate situation on a lot of our lands than some of our sister agencies.

Dr. LOWENTHAL. And those other Federal land management agencies, they have more comprehensive and clearer regulations covering the development of non-Federal oil and gas operations. Is that not true?

Mr. GUERTIN. Yes, that is correct, Congressman.

Dr. LOWENTHAL. So that is maybe the National Park Service, National Forest Service, and so forth.

Specifically, what does the National Park Service currently require of operations that the Fish and Wildlife Service does not——

Mr. GUERTIN. They require, in essence——

Dr. LOWENTHAL [continuing]. Of operators?

Mr. GUERTIN. They require, in essence, a permit, they require some type of surety bond or safeguards, moving forward, in case there are damages down the road. They also require the operator to work with them on siting and avoidance and mitigation measures, as well.

Dr. LOWENTHAL. I think you mentioned in your testimony that many States do not have—or have very minimum kinds of surety bonds that cost the Fish and Wildlife Service extensive amounts of money when a bond—I think it was in the State of Mississippi— was only about $10,000, and the costs ended up being far greater than that. And the taxpayers had to cover that cost. Is that not so?

Mr. GUERTIN. Yes, Congressman. It can vary, State by State. There have been cases where we have had to, and the taxpayers have had to pay pretty significant damages for remediation and cleanup.

Dr. LOWENTHAL. Well, you know, I think my colleagues here on both sides of the aisle really care about being fiscally responsible. And so I would hope that any final rule would also keep the taxpayers from being on the hook for the millions of dollars for abandoned oil and gas infrastructure and contamination cleanup. Is that one of the Service's goals?

Mr. GUERTIN. Yes, Congressman. And, above all, our goal is that we want to protect the taxpayers and sports-person's investment in the National Wildlife Refuge System that has been——

Dr. LOWENTHAL. Well, thank you. It just seems to me that the Service is finally addressing a long-recognized problem, a real problem, that the Refuge System has repeatedly borne serious degradations to refuge resources from leaks and spills; inadequate plugging, as you pointed out in your prepared testimony; abandonment, which you pointed out; and reclamation. And the Service is now taking the necessary steps to apply a consistent and reasonable—hopefully, reasonable—set of regulatory and management controls over oil and gas activities in the Refuge System in order to protect the public's surface interests.

I think, in conclusion, that this is acting in a fiscally responsible manner. And I thank you for beginning that process. And I yield back.

Dr. FLEMING. The gentleman yields back. The Chair now recognizes Mr. McAllister.

Mr. MCALLISTER. Thank you, Mr. Chairman. Mr. Guertin, in 2007 the Government Accountability Office recommended that the Service hire 32 refuge oil and gas specialists, 7 regional coordinators, and a 6-member mineral regional team. How many of those positions are currently filled?

Mr. GUERTIN. We have currently filled about four or five of the regional coordinators. We have trained over 200 employees on oil and gas procedures and regulations and policies in the System, Congressman.

Mr. MCALLISTER. OK. But how many of these actual recommendations have been filled?

Mr. GUERTIN. We have hired—the first recommendation, we have hired four people in the regional offices, of the seven. And then, of the 32 you have mentioned, we have probably filled about 15 to 20 of those positions, but we have also trained an additional 200 employees in the larger regulatory framework in working on oil and gas projects.

Mr. MCALLISTER. So those are current employees that you just sent back for retraining, or additional?

Mr. GUERTIN. Yes, sir.

Mr. MCALLISTER. OK. So, in the past 8 years, the Service has hired less than 25 percent, according to our numbers, of what the GAO recommended, including one licensed petroleum engineer. What are your hiring plans in the future?

Mr. GUERTIN. Congressman, we are currently evaluating our portfolio of program management, going forward. The President's budget for 2015 does include some increases for the Refuge System and our ecological services program. We are putting a priority on energy development processes within the Fish and Wildlife Service, and trying to get after these at a landscape scale with all of our programs.

We can't really talk about the internal formulation of the 2016 budget yet, but we are pursuing a vision which puts a premium on energy development and positions for energy in that area.

And also note, as you know, Congressman, all of the agencies went through some pretty significant trim in the budget the last couple of years. We are actually down several hundred employees, overall, with the Fish and Wildlife Service. But rather than just willy nilly fill those positions with whoever anyone wants, we are targeting energy portfolio program management positions as we re-build the workforce out there in the field stations.

Mr. MCALLISTER. I completely agree, and appreciate that, taking the time. But, I mean, 8 years? I think if I had to take an 8-year hiring process in my business, we would be out of business.

And also, the GAO recommended in 2003 that the Service establish an inventory of oil and gas wells and infrastructure on refuge lands. What is the status of that comprehensive inventory?

Mr. GUERTIN. We have actually completed a pilot, which targeted the States with the largest amount of National Wildlife Refuges with oil and gas development on the Mississippi and Louisiana. That is not ready for public preview at this point, but we would be glad to give you or your staff a kind of off-the-record update on that, if it would be helpful to you. And then we envision moving forward with the full study analysis over the coming fiscal year, as well.

Mr. MCALLISTER. So that is the pilot program that you are doing right now that will eventually become a national tracking system for——

Mr. GUERTIN. Yes, and we have targeted the States with the pre-ponderance of units of the Refuge System with oil and gas develop-ment on them. And that is an internal document at this point. But, again, if you are interested, we would offer to come up and brief you on that.

Mr. MCALLISTER. Absolutely. I would appreciate it if you could give it to the office whenever you have the chance.

Since the Service has a legitimate concern about abandoned wells and orphaned infrastructure equipment, why not confine your new regulations just to addressing these problems?

Mr. GUERTIN. We are envisioning taking a look at the larger landscape out there. We are also trying to be more strategic and look down the road 10, 15, 20 years. Because of the burgeoning in-terest in energy development in the country here, a lot of the emerging technologies, new formations being discovered, we are really looking at where we think we are going to be 15 or 20 years from now, and our vision points us that we need to be much more bigger-thinking about this, and look at the entirety of the Refuge System, and take that strategic stance.

Mr. MCALLISTER. So how many qualified oil and gas inspectors work for the Fish and Wildlife Service?

Mr. GUERTIN. Mr. Chairman, I think we have about 10 or 12, but I will confirm that for the record for you.

Mr. MCALLISTER. Ten or twelve to cover the entire Nation?

Mr. GUERTIN. Yes, sir.

Mr. MCALLISTER. OK. So, just to address the two case studies you cite in your testimony involving abandoned rigs and equipment, why not confine any future regulations to addressing what is, obviously, the largest problem facing the Service, and that is abandoned energy equipment?

Mr. GUERTIN. We are going to evaluate the abandoned energy equipment as part of this advanced notice of proposed rulemaking. We envision looking at several aspects of the issue, including the surety bond we talked about before, access fees, if any, looking at public access and other uses. And we are certainly going to take to heart your comments on this larger issue within this kind of umbrella here of this abandoned equipment, because that is one that directly adds to our maintenance backlog woes, as an agency.

Mr. MCALLISTER. Well, I appreciate that. And just to go back, as Congressman Duncan had said, previously in your testimony your reference to the GAO report was that the Service was largely ignored. So you are aware in 2007 the GAO report also stated, ''We believe it is for Congress, not the Department of the Interior, to weigh the needs of the refuge lands and interests of mineral owners, and, ultimately, to determine what oversight authority would be appropriate.'' If you want to follow the GAO's recommendations, why not just submit legislation to Congress, rather than continue with more overreach and government regulation?

Mr. GUERTIN. Sure, Congressman, that is a great question. You know, our administration and our agency believe that the refuge organic legislation and the Refuge Improvement Act gives us that authority. But we certainly want to continue this conversation with yourself, the Chairman, and other leaders here on Capitol Hill. We are all after the same thing here: that is a vibrant energy economy for America, while safeguarding this beautiful natural resource that we have so all Americans can hunt and fish and recreate in the great out-of-doors. So we will continue to partner with the leaders up here on congressional hill to pursue that vision.

Mr. MCALLISTER. Appreciate your time. Sorry, Chairman, for overstaying my time.

Dr. FLEMING. The gentleman yields back. And I think we would like to have another round of questions. I haven't had a crack at Mr. Knudson yet. And so, I would like to ask you, sir, of course, some good questions here.

The only reason that I can ascertain that Fish and Wildlife and other services would find a need to regulate oil and gas—something that was not really done in the past—on refuges would be, obviously, that States such as Alaska have no regulations that protect human health, groundwater, surface water, public safety, at the oil and gas operations at such places as Kenai National Wildlife Refuge. Am I wrong about that, sir?

Mr. KNUDSON. No, if I am understanding the question, I mean, if——

Dr. FLEMING. I guess to better phrase the question, does Alaska have regulations?

Mr. KNUDSON. Yes, sir. If you talk to any private operator, they would confirm vehemently that we are paying a lot of attention to their activities. Thank you.

Dr. FLEMING. Yes, sir.

Mr. KNUDSON. Yes.

Dr. FLEMING. And those regulations would be there to protect humans, their health, the groundwater, surface water, and public safety.

So, again, if Alaska has regulatory powers and abilities, and expertise—by the way, how many regulatory inspectors are there in Alaska for such oil and gas wells?

Mr. KNUDSON. Well, I would be afraid to tell you that total number, because that could be controversial back home, but it is hundreds.

Dr. FLEMING. Hundreds, OK, as opposed to Fish and Wildlife that has—you said, Mr. Guertin—10 or 11?

Mr. GUERTIN. I think it is about 10 or 12, Mr. Chairman.

Dr. FLEMING. OK.

Mr. GUERTIN. I am going to confirm that.

Dr. FLEMING. And so, it seems to me that the expertise lies with the State here. So, I guess I am sort of wondering here. Why is it that the Federal Government—is there something unique about the Federal Government that means it can somehow do a better job at regulating such activities as oil and gas within States who have developed that expertise over the years?

I was just speaking with folks back home in Louisiana. They tell me that Louisiana does an excellent job. And I think even the Fish and Wildlife Service would concede that fact. So it just seems to me that we are only adding just yet another layer of regulatory bureaucracy to the one that we already have.

Another question. Are there major gaps in Alaskan State law that demand that the Federal Government now implement a new series of regulatory requirements? So, yes, you have regulations, you have perhaps hundreds of inspectors. But are there perhaps some gaps that we haven't, that we are not covering there in Alaska?

Mr. KNUDSON. No sir. I am not aware of any gaps that have been identified. You know, we have primacy for air and water. We have an oil and gas conservation commission that works on the infrastructure related to the drilling operation. You know, soup to nuts.

Dr. FLEMING. And does the State of Alaska have a requirement to inspect those 800 wells at Kenai National Wildlife Refuge? And how often do those inspections occur? And what is the nature of those inspections?

Mr. KNUDSON. Sir, I believe it is 80 wells on Kenai. I think it is 80, not 800. But——

Dr. FLEMING. OK, somebody dropped an extra zero in on me here, so I apologize.

Mr. KNUDSON. Yes, it is still, you know, it is a lot. We will take credit for that. And it is producing very significant amounts of energy.

The frequency of inspection varies on the operation, depending on the operation. But as much as two times a year. And, depending on the activity in development, it could be more frequent than that.

Dr. FLEMING. Now, what about abandoned wells? Now, in Louisiana, I was told today, that there is a well orphan fund and regulations that provide for that, that if someone goes bankrupt, they abandon the well, you can't find the person who operated that, who did the original drilling, the State has a fund for that. There is also a bond, as we have already discussed. What about Alaska?

Mr. KNUDSON. We do not have any privately operated wells that have been abandoned or currently don't have a sponsor for dismantlement, repair, and restoration. The only operator we have a problem with on that front is the Federal Government.

Dr. FLEMING. Yes. Just again, did I hear you correctly? You showed a picture here a moment ago, and it was—as it turns out, it was BLM that actually created that disaster?

Mr. KNUDSON. Yes.

Dr. FLEMING. OK. So——

Mr. KNUDSON. We have those throughout the State. And it is not just oil and gas activity. But there are almost 100 wells on the North Slope—in particular, on the National Petroleum Reserve— that have been, effectively, abandoned and not appropriately dismantled by the Federal Government.

Dr. FLEMING. So the statement that, "I am from the Federal Government, I am here to help you" may not apply always in the case of Alaska.

Mr. KNUDSON. If they are writing checks, we know where to send the money.

Dr. FLEMING. Yes, sir. I think I yield back, and I yield to the gentleman, Mr. Sablan.

Mr. SABLAN. Well, thank you very much, Mr. Chairman. I am really learning a lot here today, also. Eventually, I will probably know as much about abandoned wells and orphaned wells as I do about red snappers and, what was that other? The Lacey Act or something. I mean that in all honesty, too.

But, Mr. Guertin, again, I come back to you, because some of the witnesses today attempt to argue, essentially, that the Service does not have the regulatory authority to protect public trust resources on National Wildlife Refuge. Could you provide some clarity on that point today, please?

Mr. GUERTIN. Yes, Congressman. We believe that the organic legislation in the National Wildlife Refuge Improvement Act of 1997 gives us the authority and mandates that we manage the National Wildlife Refuge System with a priority placed on conservation and its wildlife values. It also charges us with developing a series of step-down management plans for each individual unit of the Wildlife Refuge System to, again, put a priority on conservation and wildlife management.

And we are going to cite that as authority moving forward to give us this impetus to partner with industry, with States, Tribes, private land owners, the energy economy, to work with them to get access to their property that underlies the National Wildlife Refuge System, but partner with them on the siting, placement, and timing of when they conduct operations to avoid and minimize significant impacts to the Nation's investment on the National Wildlife Refuge System.

Mr. SABLAN. OK. In the second panel, but in the written testimony, in his testimony Mr. Schutt complains about constantly shifting rules being applied to oil and gas operations at Kenai National Wildlife Refuge. Isn't the problem, though, that there are no rules? And would updating your regulations create more certainty and consistency for Mr. Schutt?

Mr. GUERTIN. There really is no current regime for us to operate under on the National Wildlife Refuge System. There are some vague executive orders and things like that. We are confident that this new regulatory framework would provide us that type of certainty for our refuge managers, as well as for the energy industry.

We recognize there are unique circumstances in the State of Alaska. There is both the ANILCA legislation, as well as ANCSA, that my colleague has talked about here, and then the special unique characteristics of the Federal-State partnership in Alaska. And we are certainly willing, moving forward, to sit down with our partners in Alaska, and talk to them seriously about what they envision as a future management regime in Alaska, and how we would operate the National Wildlife Refuge System up there, as well.

But the bottom line for us is this rulemaking, we think, will give all of the conservation partners the certainty and credibility they need, moving forward.

Mr. SABLAN. And, you know, I have been here, what, 5 years. And I just finally—I mean, maybe it is not the first time, but it is the first time I actually heard my colleagues on the other side questioning why you don't hire people consistent with—you know, I don't know whether you have the money to do that.

But talking about consistency here, because I am just learning these things, to be very honest, but on this instance of surety bonds, in Louisiana you have 10 wells, I think, for $25,000. So that is about $2,500 per well. In Mississippi, the bond is $10,000. My thought is it must be confusing for owners and operators of these wells—so many own properties in more than one State—to sort out all these different requirements, not just on the surety bonds, but I am sure there is different regulation in the several States.

So I thank you for finally—I am going to say finally—getting to do the work required or expected of you out of this GAO report. And I yield my time, Mr. Chairman.

Dr. FLEMING. The gentleman yields. Mr. McAllister, you are recognized for 5 minutes.

Mr. McALLISTER. Thank you, Mr. Chairman. Just to clarify one thing, Mr. Guertin. We are—and I am just reading through the National Wildlife Refuge System Improvement Act of 1997. And clarify me if I am not seeing it, but where anywhere in here does it talk about subsurface rights?

Mr. GUERTIN. The Refuge System Improvement Act does not specifically address subsurface rights, Congressman, you are correct in that observation. What we are citing is the larger authorities that were vested with the Fish and Wildlife Service to manage the units of the Refuge System with a priority on wildlife first and conservation, as well as the mandates in that legislation that direct us to establish these management plans, or CCPs, for each unit of the Refuge System. And that is the authority, we believe, that launches us on this rulemaking process.

Mr. McALLISTER. OK. Back one more question about the hiring of inspectors and petroleum engineers and other stuff.

Over an 8-year period of time you all haven't been able to fill these positions, but you've got the BLM sitting over there with hundreds of experts in the same business. Why not contract with them to get these services taken care of and get the problem handled, rather than continuing to push it off and blame it on budget cuts and what else? If we already have them on the payroll, why not utilize them?

Mr. GUERTIN. Certainly, Congressman, and that is the kind of feedback we welcome. We will certainly take that to heart, and approach BLM to see if they have any capacities that could help us in our endeavor moving forward, as well.

Mr. McALLISTER. Now to Mr. Alaska.

[Laughter.]

Mr. McALLISTER. He just walked in. You know, this is probably one of the major frustrations I have up here with Congress and with our role as a government and all is, we should be more of a sounding board and more of a helpful tool to 50 States, not try to make the United States a one-State system.

I want to commend you on the information you provided from Alaska. And me, being from Louisiana, I know what it is like to be an oil and gas-producing State. Do you feel very frustrated with sitting here, having to have talks about trying to keep more regulation from going to the top of the regulation you all have already imposed upon yourself, and you don't feel like you get the support from us to help enforce what you are doing? Instead we want to try to reinvent the wheel every time we turn around and, instead, look over your shoulder?

Mr. KNUDSON. Congressman, I believe that we would politely express some frustration with that activity. And the issue is every environment, every refuge is different, has unique circumstances. So, for an agency, a national agency, to write rules that apply effectively in all 50 States and the territories would be, probably, an impossibility.

The other issue that we are facing—it is not necessarily that we are afraid of more regulation. It is conflicting regulation. So logic does not necessarily apply in the rule-writing process. That is another concern when multiple agencies are approaching the same activity, they are not necessarily all looking for the same thing.

Mr. McALLISTER. Well, I appreciate it, and I appreciate your time coming today, and I yield back my time, Mr. Chairman.

Dr. FLEMING. The gentleman yields back. Well, we think—I am sorry. Oh, I am sorry. The gentleman from Alaska just joined us. And so the Chair would like to recognize Mr. Young for 5 minutes.

Mr. YOUNG. Thank you, Mr. Chairman. I will try to make this short, because I know the witnesses have been sitting there.

But this is for Mr. Guertin. Does the Fish and Wildlife intend that this rulemaking effect will apply to Alaska?

Mr. GUERTIN. Sir, we have been talking about that during the beginning stages of——

Mr. YOUNG. Speak up, I can't hear you.

Mr. GUERTIN. We have been talking about that during the earlier stages of this hearing. We are currently envisioning the rule as applying to all of the States. We are certainly willing to hear more about the unique aspects of Alaska, particularly the organic legislation up there under ANILCA and ANCSA. We understand that creates a whole new dynamic for management. We have made no decision, moving forward, but we will use this public process to solicit feedback from——

Mr. YOUNG. With all due respect, this is not coming from the public. It is coming from you, not the public.

Mr. GUERTIN. No——

Mr. YOUNG. That is number one. But number two, what bothers me is we have a no-more clause, period. And we have an ANCSA provision, which is the law, and ANILCA, which is the law. Now, you've got a lot of hot-shot lawyers down in that Department now— too many, by the way, I have checked that out, you keep hiring. Now, they can find all kinds of arguments. But I don't want this just to end up in court, which it will, if you go forth with this rule and apply it to Alaska. I just want you to keep that in mind. That is number one.

Now, have you—you know, the Department itself has this government-to-government relationship with federally recognized Tribes. Have you communicated with any of our tribes in Alaska about these proposed rules?

Mr. GUERTIN. We are starting the outreach now. We have just reopened the comment period on the proposed notice, Mr. Chairman, and our Alaska office is reaching out to the Native corporations up there, as well as tribes. But we will redouble our efforts during this reopening of the comment period.

Mr. YOUNG. And it goes back to the Alaska Native Land Claims Act. They were guaranteed a certain amount of land, subsurface and surface, where the subsurface is beneath the lands which were there before you became a refuge. You are proposing that they have to go through certain regulations and activities before they can recover what was given to them by Congress. What authority will that come under?

Mr. GUERTIN. Well, you are talking about the old Kenai moose range?

Mr. YOUNG. That is right.

Mr. GUERTIN. Adopted into the——

Mr. YOUNG. And Doyon.

Mr. GUERTIN. And Doyon. And, again, we are envisioning now, through this proposed rulemaking, taking a lot of public input——

Mr. YOUNG. Let me stop there. What public? Are you going to hear from the Sierra Club? You are going to hear from Save the Earth Club? Are you going to listen and give credit to those that live there, and were guaranteed by Congress the right to develop their resources for their social and economic ability or are you going to listen to a bunch of jackasses from societies that don't even live there? Who are you going to listen to?

Mr. GUERTIN. Well, we are not telling them, through this rule-making, that they do not have access to their oil and rights. We recognize that, and have made that clear for the record.

Mr. YOUNG. If I shut that door, sir, and lock it, you still have access if you have a key. But when I take the key away from you, you don't have access. Is that correct?

Mr. GUERTIN. Yes.

Mr. YOUNG. Now, if you have regulations and have stipulations that makes it impossible for people who were guaranteed, under ANCSA and ANILCA, their rights to land, because you have taken the key away from them, is that a right?

Mr. GUERTIN. Well, we are not necessarily talking about taking the key away from them, though.

Mr. YOUNG. You are going to make the key this big, OK? And the hole is going to be this big. That is not the intent. That is why I would say I would suggest respectfully that your organization—and thank God we're through with your administration—think about previous laws that impose restrictions on what was guaranteed under other laws when you take away that key.

And I am not talking about you personally, I am just telling the whole God-darn blessed Fish and Wildlife Department has got this idea, again, they are God, and Congress doesn't count. I sat on this committee and watched us pass these laws guaranteeing this, and I have agencies saying, "Oh, that is not what Congress meant. This is what we are going to do," going against the will of the Congress and hurting the people that we are supposed to be helping.

And I hope you take this back downtown, explain my frustration. And they say, "Oh, that is just Young." It is not. This is America, not a bunch of dictators dictating through agencies. They are taking away the rights of individuals this Congress said they had. And that is what you are trying to do by who and where this came from.

Now, and last question. Who brought up this harebrained idea? Whose idea was it?

Mr. GUERTIN. Do you mean the idea of launching the ANPR?

Mr. YOUNG. No, the idea about taking away the rights and not allowing people to drill on these refuges. What gives you the right that they can bring up this idea? Where did it come from?

Mr. GUERTIN. Mr. Chairman, again, we are not talking about denying them access to their minerals.

Mr. YOUNG. Where did this restriction come from? Whose idea was it?

Mr. GUERTIN. I can't point to a single individual, Mr. Chairman.

Mr. YOUNG. Which group?

Mr. GUERTIN. Well, this is based on guidance we have gotten from the General Accountability Office for us to improve the management of the oil and gas program on the National Wildlife Refuge System. And then, within the Fish and Wildlife Service, I, as Deputy Director for Policy, have certainly enforced that——

Mr. YOUNG. I would like to have a report from your Department of any correspondence from any other interest groups, and where this originated from. I am requesting that, Mr. Chairman, respectfully. I want to know where this stinking thing arose from, when you take away the right or take away and not let the key fit the lock. I want to know where it came from.

Mr. Chairman, my time is up.

Dr. FLEMING. The gentleman yields back. And I want to thank the panel today, panel one. You are now dismissed, and of course, we may have questions. We will keep the record open for 10 days. And I will ask the second panel to step forward.

[Pause.]

Dr. FLEMING. We are now ready for our second panel, which includes Mr. Dan Naatz—is that correct?

Mr. NAATZ. Naatz.

Dr. FLEMING. Naatz. Mr. Naatz, Vice President, Independent Petroleum Association of America; Mr. J. Davis Powell, Board Member, Louisiana Chapter, National Association of Royalty Owners; Mr. Ethan Schutt, Vice President for Land and Energy Development for the Cook Inlet Region Corporation; Mr. Noah Matson, Vice President for Landscape Conservation and Climate Adaptation, Defenders of Wildlife.

Your written testimony will appear in full in the hearing record, so I ask that you keep your oral statements to 5 minutes, as outlined in our invitation letter to you, and under Rule 4(a).

Our microphones are not automatic, so please press a button, make sure the tip of the microphone is close to your mouth.

Our timing lights, again, very simple. You have 5 minutes to give your oral testimony. You will be 4 minutes under green, 1 minute under yellow, and when it turns red we ask you to quickly conclude, if you haven't already, so we can move on to the next testimonies, and also to answer questions.

Mr. Naatz, you are now recognized, sir, for 5 minutes to present your testimony on behalf of the Independent Petroleum Association of America.

STATEMENT OF DAN NAATZ, VICE PRESIDENT, INDEPENDENT PETROLEUM ASSOCIATION OF AMERICA

Mr. NAATZ. Thank you, Mr. Chairman, and members of the subcommittee. My name is Dan Naatz, and I am the Vice President of Federal Resources and Political Affairs for the Independent Petroleum Association of America. IPAA represents thousands of independent oil and natural gas explorers and producers, as well as the service and supply industries that support their efforts.

America's independent producers develop 95 percent of American oil and natural gas wells, produce 54 percent of American oil, and 85 percent of the Nation's natural gas. IPAA and our members are concerned with the nature of the advanced notice of proposed rulemaking on non-Federal—and I stress non-Federal—oil and gas development within the National Wildlife Refuge System.

Unfortunately, this rule is similar to many other rules that we have seen come from the Obama administration: it is a solution in search of a problem. Ultimately, we believe, the imposition of additional regulations on non-Federal oil and gas development within the National Wildlife Refuge System is unnecessary, has not been justified by the Fish and Wildlife Service, is constrained by the bounds on the agency's authority, and will only result in duplicative layers of regulatory oversight.

After conducting a thorough analysis of the intent and scope of the rule, we believe this rulemaking is premature. As I mentioned earlier, the Obama administration has consistently sought to regulate areas that are already heavily regulated in the oil and gas industry.

One of our biggest concerns with this rulemaking is the lack of jurisdiction we believe the Fish and Wildlife Service may have regarding this matter. The agency has not identified a specific statutory grant of authority to issue this.

As we have discussed previously, the committee has heard regarding the GAO reports that GAO again recommended that the Fish and Wildlife Service work with the Department of the Interior's Office of the Solicitor to seek from Congress any necessary additional authority over outstanding mineral rights. As late as 2007 the GAO surmised, ''We do not believe that DOI has adequate information on which to base this claim.'' In particular, the Fish and Wildlife Service has yet to publicly clarify the extent of its current authority over private minerals rights.

Again, other members of the subcommittee have already referenced this, but the GAO continues further in writing by saying, ''We believe it is for Congress, not DOI, to weigh the needs of the refuge lands and the interests of mineral owners and, ultimately, to determine what oversight authority would be appropriate.''

Since 2007, the agency has not publicly clarified its authority in this regard. For a rule that we believe will provide little to no environmental benefit, the first step from the Fish and Wildlife Service should be clarification of their authority.

While we understand that the Fish and Wildlife Service appears to believe that the current regulatory structure leads to an uncertain and inconsistent regulatory environment for oil and gas operators on refuges, IPAA members do not share this view. To the contrary, the existing regulatory structure provides operators and mineral estate owners with the flexibility needed to develop mineral interests consistent with their legal rights.

Much of what Fish and Wildlife Service contemplates in this rulemaking seems to suggest that there are insufficient regulations in place to protect refuge resources. We believe that sufficient State regulations already exist to protect these areas.

Unlike other Federal land programs, the National Fish and Wildlife Refuge System is unique, in terms of how the United States came to acquire the land. Each refuge carries a different acquisition history, which means that the Federal Government's interest in and administration of each refuge must vary. Various refuge lands came with different easements and access exemptions, different mineral extraction rights, and different obligations to facilitate oil and gas development.

The Fish and Wildlife Service personnel must also engage in differing levels of intergovernmental cooperation from refuge to refuge. Each refuge is further subject to different conservation plans. In 1997, Congress enacted the National Wildlife Refuge System Improvement Act, amending the original Refuge Act, and mandating that the Fish and Wildlife Service develop comprehensive conservation plans, CCPs, for each National Wildlife Refuge.

Adoption of a CCP involves a deliberation process that includes a lengthy public comment period. Congress directed the Fish and Wildlife Service to manage each refuge in a manner consistent with the completed CCP, and to revise the plan at any time, if conditions that affect a specific refuge are deemed to have changed significantly. These extensive proceedings for developing refuge-specific CCPs underscores that a one-size-fits-all approach to oil and gas regulation is incompatible with the needs of any specific refuge.

Mr. Chairman, my written comments go into far more detail on many of these issues. But, for the sake of time, I will conclude my comments.

IPAA appreciates the opportunity to appear before you today, and we will be happy to answer any questions.

[The prepared statement of Mr. Naatz follows:]

PREPARED STATEMENT OF DAN NAATZ, VICE PRESIDENT OF FEDERAL RESOURCES & REGULATORY AFFAIRS, THE INDEPENDENT PETROLEUM ASSOCIATION OF AMERICA

The Independent Petroleum Association of America (IPAA) represents thousands of independent oil and natural gas explorers and producers, as well as the service and supply industries that support their efforts. Independent producers develop 95 percent of American oil and natural gas wells, produce 54 percent of American oil and produce 85 percent of American natural gas. The average independent has been in business for 26 years and employs 12 full-time and 3 part-time employees. IPAA's members are truly the face of small business in the oil and natural gas industry and support more than two million direct jobs in the United States.

This testimony is in regards to an advanced notice of proposed rulemaking (ANOPR) on Non-Federal Oil and Gas Development within the National Wildlife Refuge System (NWRF) that the U.S. Fish and Wildlife Service (FWS) released in February. IPAA is concerned with the nature of this advanced notice of proposed rulemaking and we submitted extensive comments that describe the challenges with the ANOPR in late April. Unfortunately, this rule is similar to many other rules that we have seen come from the Obama administration; it's a solution in search of a problem. Ultimately, we believe the imposition of additional regulations on non-Federal oil and gas development within the National Wildlife Refuge System is unnecessary, has not been justified by FWS, is constrained by the bounds on FWS' legal authority, and will only result in duplicative layers of regulatory oversight.[1] We requested that FWS refrain from future rulemaking in this regard in our official comments.

After doing a thorough analysis of the intent and scope of the rule, we believe this rulemaking is premature. As we mentioned in the introduction, the Obama administration has consistently sought to regulate areas that are already regulated. Another example of duplicative regulation is the Bureau of Land Management's hydraulic fracturing and well stimulation rule that attempts to solve an issue of groundwater contamination that simple does not exist. Administration officials, academics, and experts in the field have all testified that hydraulic fracturing, which has been done over two million times, does not contaminate groundwater.

In regards to this particular advanced notice, IPAA has many questions regarding FWS' authority to regulate development within refuge boundaries. Mineral owners have the legal right to explore for and extract oil and gas from their mineral estates, a fact FWS recognizes.[2] Mineral rights represent a dominant estate, taking precedence over other rights associated with property, including surface rights.[3] As a result, FWS is limited in its authority to inhibit operations, including horizontal drilling from private lands, to access minerals under a refuge, and we would expect FWS to adhere to the legal bounds of its authority.[4]

---

[1] Domestic oil and gas production from lands within the National Wildlife Refuge System is also consistent with Federal energy policy, as set forth in the Comprehensive National Energy Strategy announced by the U.S. Department of Energy in April of 1998, the Energy Policy and Conservation Act, 42 U.S.C. § 6201, et seq., the National Energy Policy, Executive Order No. 13212, 66 Fed. Reg. 28,357 (May 18, 2001), and the Energy Policy Act of 2005, Pub. L. 109–58, 119 Stat. 594.

[2] See, e.g., Nat'l Wildlife Refuge Sys., Oil & Gas FAQs, available at: http://www.fws.gov/refuges/oil-and-gas/faqs.html.

[3] See, e.g., Gerrity Oil & Gas Corp. v. Magness, 946 P.2d 913, 926–27 (Colo. 1997); DuLaney v. Okla. State Dep't of Health, 868 P.2d 676, 680 (Okla. 1993); Merriman v. XTO Energy, Inc., 407 S.W.3d 244, 249 (Tex. 2013).

[4] Nor is the scope of FWS' authority uniform across refuge lands. On each individual refuge, the issue of mineral ownership must be addressed on a case-by-case basis since the law of mineral rights varies among States, the government's land acquisition contracts contain different mineral rights reservations, and contract interpretation may depend on the legal rules in place at the time of the contract. See, e.g., Petro-Hunt, LLC v. United States, 365 F.3d 385, 393 (5th Cir. 2004) (concerning private parties' efforts to quiet title to mineral rights in federally owned

Continued

One of our biggest concerns is the lack of jurisdiction that we believe the Service may have with this rulemaking. FWS has not identified a specific statutory grant of authority to issue this ANOPR.[5] In a 2003 report, the Government Accountability Office (''GAO'') recommended that FWS work with the Department of the Interior's Office of the Solicitor to seek from Congress any necessary additional authority over outstanding and reserved mineral rights.[6] In response, the Department of the Interior professed its belief that it had the requisite authority to oversee oil and gas development. As late as 2007, however, GAO disagreed:

> [W]e do not believe that DOI has adequate information on which to base this claim. In particular, *FWS . . . has yet to publicly clarify the extent of its current authority over private mineral rights.* We continue to believe that such information is necessary for DOI to adequately inform the Congress regarding the need for additional authority. Moreover, *we believe it is for Congress, not DOI, to weigh the needs of the refuge lands and the interests of mineral owners and, ultimately, to determine what oversight authority would be appropriate.*[7]

Since 2007, FWS has not publicly clarified its authority in this regard. Again, for a rule that we believe will provide zero environmental benefit, we believe the first step from the FWS should be clarification of their authority before they proceed with a formal rulemaking.

Overregulation without environmental benefit undoubtedly steers investment away from those properties. We have seen similar occurrences happen with over-regulation of Federal minerals. By having application for permit to drill (APD) times that nearly triple[8] those of State processing applications, investment has been driven off of Federal minerals. An EIA report shows this decline.[9] In the same respect, FWS also fails to provide a legitimate purpose and need for additional regulation in regards to non-Federal minerals on National Wildlife Refuge Lands. In particular, there is insufficient data to support the necessity of a rulemaking at this time. While FWS has begun to collect information on ''Oil-Related Leaks and Spills on National Wildlife Refuges,''[10] that data set is limited, and the information reflects only the identity of the substance leaked and the quantity discharged. It does not conclude that such spills have had an adverse impact to the refuges or that operators categorically fail to address and remediate spills. To the contrary, FWS personnel have indicated they are working positively with operators.[11] Combined with this data collection, in April 2012, FWS introduced a management program handbook: ''Management of Oil and Gas Activities on National Wildlife Refuge System Lands.'' Insufficient time has passed to allow either FWS or oil and gas operators to determine the efficacy of that tool. A rulemaking premised on these same untested management guidelines is premature. We urge the FWS to complete an analysis of gaps that may exist in their current practices before moving forward with another unnecessary and costly rulemaking to the American taxpayers.

While we understand that FWS appears to believe that the current regulatory structure leads to ''an uncertain and inconsistent regulatory environment for oil and gas operators on refuges,''[12] our members do not share this concern. To the contrary, as discussed further below, the existing regulatory structure provides opera-

---

land). *See also* discussion *infra* p. 4 and notes 13–14. With so many variables, any regulatory regime would be confusing, lacking in uniform applicability, and potentially subject to perpetual legal challenges.

[5] In the Federal Register notice regarding this proposed rulemaking, FWS only points generally to the Property and Commerce Clauses of the United States Constitution and the National Wildlife Refuge System Administration Act of 1966, as amended, for its authority to promulgate these rules. 79 Fed. Reg. 10,080, 10,081 (Feb. 24, 2014).

[6] GAO, *Nat'l Wildlife Refuges: Opportunities to Improve the Mgmt. & Oversight of Oil & Gas Activities on Fed. Lands*, GAO–03–517 (Wash., DC: Aug. 28, 2003).

[7] GAO, *U.S. Fish & Wildlife Serv.: Opportunities Remain to Improve Oversight & Mgmt. of Oil & Gas Activities on Nat'l Wildlife Refuges*, GAO–07–829R (Wash., DC: June 29, 2007) (emphasis added).

[8] http://www.blm.gov/wo/st/en/prog/energy/oil_and_gas/statistics/apd_chart.html.

[9] Link from E+C Committee Web site: http://www.google.com/url?sa=t&rct=j&q= &esrc=s&source=web&cd=2&ved=0CDIQFjAB&url=http%3A%2F%2Fenergycommerce.house.gov %2Fsites%2Frepublicans.energycommerce.house.gov%2Ffiles% 2F20140410CRS-US-crude-oil-natural-gas-production-federal-non-federal-areas.pdf&ei=P7VzU-LIG4_LsASD9oDgBA&usg=AFQ jCNGCL4GQlkDec1ymQxNi7FkeO0HpOw&sig2=6uUDn8sbVaoF3ApJUAyWnw.

[10] *See* U.S. Fish & Wildlife Serv., ''Oil-Related Leaks & Spills on Nat'l Wildlife Refuges'' provided to the Committee on Natural Resources (undated).

[11] *Id.* at 1.

[12] 79 Fed. Reg, at 10,081.

tors and mineral estate owners with the flexibility needed to develop mineral interests consistent with their legal rights.

Much of what FWS contemplates in this rulemaking seems to suggest that there are insufficient regulations in place to protect refuge resources. We believe that sufficient regulations already exist to protect Refuge resources.

Federal regulations already apply to development of non-Federal minerals (*see, e.g.,* 40 CFR 60, 61, 63), as do State and tribal regulations. FWS suggests that additional regulation is necessary because State oil and gas commissions have a different mission, suggesting that they do not adequately address environmental concerns. This contention is incorrect. In every State in which FWS has identified active and inactive wells,[13] oil and gas commissions have adopted regulations that protect the environment through comprehensive drilling, development, and production standards; setbacks; ground water protection measures; financial assurance requirements; spill reporting; and reclamation requirements.[14]

Unlike other Federal lands programs, the National Wildlife Refuge System is unique in terms of how the United States came to acquire the land. Each Refuge carries a different acquisition history, which means that the Federal Government's interest in, and administration of, each Refuge must vary. For example, the Lower Hatchie National Wildlife Refuge in Tennessee was acquired by deeded conveyance from a private owner and subject to existing easements for pipelines, public highways and roads at the time of the government's acquisition.[15] Nearby Reelfoot National Wildlife Refuge, conversely, is comprised of 2,300 acres that FWS owns outright and 7,860 acres that the State of Tennessee leases to the United States.[16] In addition to differences in ownership conditions, certain Refuges are subject to unique management mandates; the National Wildlife Refuge System in Alaska, for instance, is subject to a unique statutory regime under the Alaska Native Claims Settlement Act[17] and the Alaska National Interest Lands Conservation Act of 1980.[18] Various refuge lands come with different easement and access exceptions, different mineral extraction rights, and different obligations to facilitate oil and gas development. FWS personnel must also engage in differing levels of intergovernmental cooperation from refuge to refuge.

Each Refuge is further subject to a different conservation plan. In 1997, Congress enacted the National Wildlife Refuge System Improvement Act,[19] amending the Refuge Act and mandating that FWS develop comprehensive conservation plans ("CCP") for each national wildlife refuge.[20] Adoption of a CCP involves a deliberation process that includes a public comment period. Congress directed FWS to manage each refuge in a manner consistent with the completed CCP and to revise the plan at any time if conditions that affect the Refuge are deemed to have changed significantly.[21] The development of the CCP often includes a public NEPA process resulting in the preparation of an Environmental Assessment. For several refuges, the CCP also requires adoption of an additional Management Plan. These extensive proceedings for developing refuge-specific CCPs underscores that a "one-size-fits-all" approach to oil and gas regulation is incompatible with the needs of any specific refuge.

Finally, FWS' own data refutes the conclusion that oil and gas production has impacted refuges universally. The National Wildlife Refuge System includes more than 560 refuges, 38 wetland management districts and other protected areas encompassing 150 million acres of land and water from the Caribbean to the remote Pacific. There is at least one national wildlife refuge in every State and territory. Yet FWS' Fact Sheet on "Non-Federal Oil and Gas Development on National Wildlife Refuge System Lands" recognizes that half of all active wells are found on just *five refuges.* Information FWS compiled [22] shows that despite the fact that the System contains over 600 protected areas, only 46 have known and confirmed active wells, and 23 of those have five or fewer active wells.

---

[13] *See* discussion of this data, *infra* p. 5.
[14] *See, e.g.,* La. Admin. Code tit. 43: IX, XI, XIII, XVIII, XIX (2013); Okla. Admin. Code §§ 165:10–1–1 (2013), *et seq.*
[15] *See Burlison* v. *United States*, 533 F.3d 419 (6th Cir. 2008).
[16] *See Bunch* v. *Hodel*, 793 F.2d 129 (6th Cir. 1986).
[17] Pub. L. 92–203, 85 Stat. 688 (1971).
[18] Pub. L. 96–487, 94 Stat. 2371 (1980).
[19] Pub. L. 105–57, 111 Stat. 1252–1260 (codified as amended at 16 U.S.C. §§ 668dd–668ee).
[20] 16 U.S.C. § 668dd(e)(1)(A).
[21] 16 U.S.C. § 668dd(e)(1)(E).
[22] FWS provided this information to the Committee on Natural Resources with a disclaimer noting limitations on the source of the information, including an explanation that "[e]rrors are inherent in the collection of data on thousands of wells."

38

IPAA's member companies are committed to finding creative solutions to problems that exist within the scope of oil and natural gas development, but we believe this advance notice falls short of providing real environmental benefit. IPAA's member companies are committed to being smart, responsible environmental stewards of the land, but only when the regulation solves a gap in regulation.

Thank you for the opportunity to participate in today's hearing.

———

Dr. FLEMING. Thank you, Mr. Naatz, for your testimony.

Mr. Powell, you are now recognized for 5 minutes to present testimony on behalf of the National Association of Royalty Owners.

STATEMENT OF J. DAVIS POWELL, BOARD MEMBER, NATIONAL ASSOCIATION OF ROYALTY OWNERS, LOUISIANA CHAPTER

Mr. POWELL. Thank you. Chairman Fleming, Ranking Member Sablan, members of the subcommittee, thank you for the invitation to be here today. My name is Davis Powell, from Shreveport, Louisiana, and I am speaking on behalf of the National Association of Royalty Owners, also known as NARO. I currently serve on the Board of Directors for the Louisiana Chapter of NARO. We have entered a statement for the record, and I will briefly touch on a few critical points here.

NARO estimates that there are between 8.5 to 12 million royalty owners nationwide who receive income from the production of their oil, natural gas, or other private mineral interests. NARO's average member is about 60 years old, widowed, and receives around $500 a month in royalty income. About 70 percent of the minerals in the United States are owned by individual citizens. In 2012, roughly 77 percent of the oil and 81 percent of the natural gas produced on shore came from these privately owned minerals. For this reason, royalty owners are vital to U.S. energy security and to the economy that depends on domestic oil and gas production.

NARO would like to offer four basic tenants for consideration by the U.S. Fish and Wildlife Service as it works to improve management of oil and gas operations on the Refuge System.

First, it is a well-established point of law in all jurisdictions of the United States that the rights of the mineral estate are dominant over the rights of the surface estate. The law's recognition of the dominant mineral estate has been found essential, since any other priority would risk the complete devaluation of mineral rights. Existing regulations maintain that the Service operations should not be applied so as to contravene or nullify rights vested in holders of mineral interests on refuge lands. The Service's own manual states that it must provide for the exercise of non-Federal oil and gas rights, while protecting resources to the maximum extent possible. This recognition of dominant private mineral interest is critical, and must not change.

The second tenant we offer for consideration is that any further regulation by the Service should not unreasonably restrict access to the mineral estate in a way that would essentially make development uneconomic. Courts have held that Federal agencies cannot impose conditions of approval that violate this tenant. Further, courts continue to recognize that, inherent in the ownership of mineral rights is also the right to use as much of the surface as reasonably necessary to extract and produce the minerals. The Service must not develop a regulatory avenue to develop the minerals in theory, but which actually creates an economic firewall to development in reality. Also, the Service must consider all of the varied costs incurred by the oil and gas developer as a result of surface estate requirements, so that any fee structure would be fair and reasonable.

The third tenant NARO feels should be considered in this process is that the Service may not restrict oil and gas development to the point of requiring no net impact as it seeks to mitigate surface usage. The National Environmental Policy Act does not mandate particular results, and does not require agencies to elevate environmental concerns over other appropriate considerations. In addition, any environmental analysis performed must include the economic benefits to States and localities which result from the orderly development of oil and gas within a refuge.

The fourth and final tenant NARO offers for consideration is that the Service must not attempt to regulate Service activity on non-Federal lands adjacent to a refuge. Currently, horizontal drilling techniques allow for the development of much of the non-Federal mineral estate from adjacent lands without ever disturbing the Federal surface estate. In order to encourage the surface use off of refuge lands when possible, the Service should avoid any attempt to regulate exploration activity which originates from non-Federal lands.

NARO looks forward to working with the Service as it strives to improve management of oil and gas operations on the Refuge System, and working with Congress as it performs oversight of the Service's efforts. We appreciate this opportunity to appear before the subcommittee, and thank you.

[The prepared statement of Mr. Powell follows:]

PREPARED STATEMENT OF J. DAVIS POWELL, BOARD MEMBER, NATIONAL ASSOCIATION OF ROYALTY OWNERS, LOUISIANA CHAPTER, SHREVEPORT, LOUISIANA

Chairman Fleming, Ranking Member Sablan, members of the committee, it is an honor to speak with you today regarding this important issue. Thank you for the invitation.

I am Davis Powell from Shreveport, Louisiana. I speak today as a member of the Board of Directors of the Louisiana chapter of the National Association of Royalty Owners (NARO). NARO has members in all 50 States and educates and advocates for the rights of an estimated 8.5 to 12 million citizens who receive royalty income from the production of their private property—their oil and natural gas minerals.

The average NARO member is 60 years old, a widow and makes less than $500 per month in royalty income. About 70 percent of the mineral estate in the lower 48 States is owned by individual citizens. In 2012, it was estimated that roughly 77 percent of oil and 81 percent of natural gas produced onshore was produced on private property.

Of all the wells ever drilled around the world, the vast majority have been drilled in the United States—a Nation that values private ownership of minerals and that also encourages both risk and the pursuit of profit.

The United States is the only former colony that upon achieving independence, awarded the ownership of minerals to private citizens instead of to the State. This uniquely American model was suggested by Thomas Jefferson. His concept has helped make us a strong Nation and it today is enabling America's rise to become the world's dominant energy producer.

It is our understanding that the Government Accountability Office recommended that the U.S. Fish and Wildlife Service improve management and oversight of oil and gas operations on the Refuge System and clarify the Service's permitting authority of non-Federal oil and gas operations through further regulations.

This has resulted in the Service issuing an Advanced Notice of Proposed Rulemaking and Notice of Intent to Prepare an Environmental Impact Statement. On April 22 of this year, NARO submitted comments in response to the Advanced Notice. We appreciate the opportunity to elaborate on those comments here today.

It is our belief that if the Service were to continue the process of further regulating oil and gas activity on its lands, then the following four basic tenets should drive the Service's rulemaking and this subcommittee's oversight of it.

The first is that it is a well-established point of law in all jurisdictions of the United States that the rights of the mineral estate are dominant over the rights of the surface estate. The law's recognition of the mineral estate as dominant has been found essential, lest it be subrogated to any other property rights thereby risking its devaluation.

Existing Service regulations also recognize this fact and maintain that Service operations should not be "applied so as to contravene or nullify rights vested in holders of mineral interests on refuge lands" 50 CFR § 29.32. The Service's manual states that it must "[p]rovide for the exercise of non-Federal oil and gas rights while protecting [USFWS] resources to the maximum extent possible." 612 FWS Manual 2.4.B.

Supplemental information presented for the proposed rulemaking acknowledges that, "subject to State and Federal law, the mineral rights owners have the legal authority to develop oil and gas reserves." It is this group of people that NARO represents. Just as the Service has the authority to manage the public surface estate, NARO members have a dominant legal authority to access and develop their private sub-surface estate.

Second, the Service may not unreasonably restrict access to the mineral estate in a way that makes the development thereof uneconomic or unprofitable.

Courts have held that Federal agencies cannot impose stipulations or conditions of approval (COAs) that violate this tenant. See *Utah* v. *Andrus*, 486 F. Supp. 995, 1011 (D. Utah 1979); see also *Conner* v. *Burford*, 848 F.2d 1441, 1449–50 (9th Cir. 1988). Concurrent with courts' decisions discussing the dominance of the mineral estate is a requirement that a holder of mineral rights adhere to the accommodation doctrine, which provides that a mineral owner or lessee may "use as much of the surface as reasonably necessary to extract and produce the minerals" as long as that use is reasonable. *Merriman* v. *XTO Energy, Inc.,* 407 S.W.3d 244, 248–49 (Tex. 2013).

Therefore, the Service must be held to a reasonable set of regulatory management controls that does not unduly burden private mineral owners. An excessive fee structure for access onto, or across, federally owned lands will negatively affect the value of the sub-surface estate and the economic viability of development of that estate.

The Service must not develop regulatory management tools and fees that provide a regulatory avenue to develop in theory but which creates an economic firewall to development in reality.

It is important to note that expenses incurred in the development of oil and gas minerals come in many forms. A monetary fee charged by the surface estate owner would be another such expense. All of the other costs incurred by the oil and gas developer as a result of requirements by the surface estate owner also should be taken into consideration when calculating a fair and reasonable fee structure. These other costs could include the cost and time of preparation of Environmental Impact Statements and reports unique to the Federal surface estate, rights-of-way fees for pipelines and roads, and lease maintenance and operational drilling and service costs associated with lengthy application processes.

The third basic tenet which NARO feel should be considered in this process is that the Service may not unreasonably restrict oil and gas development to the point of requiring a "no net impact" on the environment as it seeks to mitigate surface impacts.

The National Environmental Policy Act (NEPA) "does not require agencies to elevate environmental concerns over other appropriate considerations." *Citizens' Comm. to Save Our Canyons* v. *U.S. Forest Serv.,* 297 F.3d 1012, 1022 (10th Cir. 2002). Instead, NEPA is a procedural statute and does not mandate particular results. *Robertson* v. *Methow Valley Citizens Council,* 490 U.S. 332, 350 (1989). As explained by the Interior Board of Land Appeals (IBLA), "NEPA does not bar actions which affect the environment, even adversely. Rather, the process assures that decisionmakers are fully apprised of likely effects of alternative courses of action so that selection of an action represents a fully informed decision." Biodiversity Conservation Alliance, 174 IBLA 1, 13–14 (2008) (citing the *Vermont Yankee* U.S. Supreme Court case).

As the IBLA observed in *Oregon Natural Resources Council,* NEPA does not direct that Federal agencies prohibit action even where environmental degradation is inevitable. 116 IBLA 355, 361 n.6 (1980). NEPA only mandates a full consideration of the environmental impact of a proposed action before undertaking it. *Nat'l Wildlife Federation,* 169 IBLA 146, 164 (2006).

As the Service undertakes its proposed rulemaking, it must ensure that it allows for a balanced review of oil and gas development proposals and assesses any negative impacts of mitigation proposals on State and private mineral rights.

The Service may not improperly elevate environmental concerns over other appropriate considerations or seek to create a set of regulations that restricts all environmental impacts on the subject lands. Any environmental NEPA analysis must also include the economic impacts to the orderly development of oil and gas within a refuge. This includes a socioeconomic analysis that details the negative impacts any restrictions will have on State and private mineral development and the impacts to local and State economies and taxes.

Fourth, the Service must not attempt to regulate surface activity on non-Federal lands adjacent to refuges.

The proposed rulemaking states that "one of the major goals of the Service in this proposed rulemaking is to ensure that operators conduct their operations in a way that minimizes impacts to natural and cultural resources when operating on a refuge, such as locating operations away from sensitive habitats for endangered and threatened species, other priority wildlife resources, ... "

One of the best ways to accomplish this goal is to encourage operators to access the sub-surface estate from adjacent non-Federal surface estates when profitable and economic to do so.

Therefore, the Service should not attempt to regulate activity that does not use the Service's surface estate.

Today, in many instances where non-Federal land is adjacent to the lower-48 refuges, horizontal drilling technology permits the development of much of the non-Federal mineral estate without disturbing the Federal surface estate. Activity originating on non-Federal surface estate and accessing the non-Federal subsurface estate should be explicitly exempted from this proposed rulemaking.

In conclusion, NARO wishes to emphasize that the Service must:

- recognize the rights of the mineral estate are dominant over the rights of the surface estate;
- allow economic and profitable access to, and development of, the mineral estate;
- balance environmental concerns with the economic development of oil and gas minerals; and
- forego any attempt to regulate surface activity on non-Federal lands adjacent to refuges.

NARO looks forward to working with the Service as it strives to improve management and oversight of oil and gas operations on the Refuge System and with Congress as it performs proper oversight of the Service's efforts.

———

Dr. FLEMING. I thank you, Mr. Powell, for your testimony. And also, welcome to Washington from the great city of Shreveport, a major city in my district.

Mr. Schutt, you are now recognized for 5 minutes to present testimony on behalf of Cook Inlet Region Corporation.

STATEMENT OF ETHAN SCHUTT, SENIOR VICE PRESIDENT, LAND AND ENERGY DEVELOPMENT, COOK INLET REGION, INCORPORATED

Mr. SCHUTT. Thank you, Mr. Chair. My name is Ethan Schutt, I am the Senior Vice President of Land and Energy Development for Cook Inlet Region, Incorporated. I would like to thank you for the invitation and opportunity to speak to you today. I also thank other members of the committee and the Ranking Member.

CIRI is one of the 12 Alaska Native regional corporations. We happen to be the corporation in and around Cook Inlet, as the name might imply. We are headquartered in Anchorage. As you have heard already in prior testimony, we are the only regional corporation with active oil and gas production from a National Wildlife Refuge. We have a long history, as provided in the written testimony that I provided to the committee already, working with the oil and gas industry in the Cook Inlet, and specifically with the Kenai National Wildlife Refuge.

I think the theme of the testimony I provided in writing is that, although the Fish and Wildlife Service says that they do not say no to the subsurface owner, they have many ways to actually go about saying no, other than to explicitly deny access or prevent oil and gas exploration and development. I provided some case study examples in my written testimony. I will assure the members of this committee that there are actually a number of other examples just in the Shadura development within the Kenai National Wildlife Refuge that I did not have space or did not feel ranked the priority of explaining to this committee.

Unfortunately, the history of the development in the Kenai is that the Fish and Wildlife Service is stepping into the role of the State of Alaska, attempting to step into the role of the private land owner, and royalty and lessor role, through this proposed rule-making.

Alaska is a well-regulated State. There are a number of steps, permitting steps, required for air, water, oil and gas-specific activities, drilling, the type of equipment, the design of the well, inspections along the way, bonding requirements required of the oil and gas operator for anything that might happen, including the reclamation of the site at the end of oil and gas production or exploration. We are well regulated. We do not need an additional layer of financial burden. We do not need an additional layer of public comment for the development of private oil and gas resources within the National Wildlife Refuge System.

As is also indicated in my pre-filed testimony, the very proposal to impose a new set of rules by the Fish and Wildlife Service upsets a very careful balance in Alaska. There are three major land owners and parties that play in Alaska, as it relates to oil and gas. That is the State of Alaska, the Alaska Native corporations, and the Federal Government.

That balance was struck at the Statehood Act first, at the Alaska Native Claims Settlement Act some 20 years later, in 1971, and then a final grand compromise was reached between conservation interests and the private interests of Alaska Native corporations, the State of Alaska, and the citizens of Alaska in ANILCA, in 1980. This proposed rulemaking usurps the role of Congress in dictating the result of that balance. That was a carefully compromised negotiation between those various parties. The very proposal to upset that upsets the balance in Alaska, where we already have very much scrutiny, very much regulation.

I have to be honest: Alaska is the place where the environmental NGO's fundraise on their Web site in opposition to our projects. That is their fundraising mechanism. It is a business. If you look at lawyers—our favorite people, including me—you know, in Alaska, if you took the number of lawyers, the environmental litigation shops would rank probably 4 out of the top 10 law firms, by number. And they raise money in opposition to these projects by filing public comments, by soliciting with pretty pictures, ''Look at the habitat that will be destroyed by this project if you allow it to go forward.'' I think that, actually, is the genesis of what Congressman Young was asking in the question, ''Who is behind this proposed rulemaking?''

I think at this point I would defer to the comments that I prefiled, and be happy to answer any questions that you might have. Thank you.

[The prepared statement of Mr. Schutt follows:]

PREPARED STATEMENT OF ETHAN G. SCHUTT, SENIOR VICE PRESIDENT, LAND AND ENERGY DEVELOPMENT, REPRESENTING COOK INLET REGION, INC.

OIL AND GAS DEVELOPMENT AND PERMITTING ON PUBLIC LANDS IN ALASKA

I am Ethan Schutt, Senior Vice President, Land and Energy Development at Cook Inlet Region, Inc. (''CIRI''). CIRI is 1 of 12 Alaska Native Regional Corporations created in 1972 under the terms of the Alaska Native Claims Settlement Act of 1971 (''ANCSA''). CIRI is the regional corporation for the geographic area of southcentral Alaska in and around the Cook Inlet. CIRI is headquartered in Anchorage and represents more than 8,200 Alaska Native shareholders and their descendants. CIRI is the largest private landowner in southcentral Alaska and owns more than 1.3 million acres of subsurface estate and more than 600,000 acres of surface land, including more than 200,000 acres of subsurface oil and gas interests within the Kenai National Wildlife Refuge (''KNWR'').

By virtue of its land holdings in the Cook Inlet, an active oil and gas basin, CIRI has a long history of participating in the oil and gas business as a lessor and royalty owner. CIRI currently has three active lessees with oil and gas exploration, development and production activities within the KNWR. This current and historical presence in the Cook Inlet oil and gas business provides us with a well-informed perspective about the oil and gas industry as it relates to Federal regulatory and land management authority, including specifically the United States Fish and Wildlife Service (''USFWS'').

An enormous amount of Alaska is owned by the Federal Government. A significant amount of that federally owned land in Alaska is categorized as National Wildlife Refuge with more than 76.5 million acres of refuge land in the aggregate. Many of the National Wildlife Refuges in Alaska were designated as such under the carefully negotiated and crafted terms of the Alaska National Interest Lands Conservation Act of 1979, commonly referred to as ''ANILCA''. Due to the circumstances and timing of Statehood and the passage of ANCSA, many Federal conservation units are intertwined with the private landholdings and interests of ANCSA corporations and with the State of Alaska. ANILCA was a grand compromise that came after statehood and ANCSA and set aside a massive geographic area in various conservation units such as National Parks and National Wildlife Refuges. But ANILCA was not drawn up in a vacuum. It was instead a carefully crafted set of compromises by and among the State of Alaska, the ANCSA corporations, and the Federal Government to accommodate often competing priorities.

Although atypical in the exact manner by which CIRI acquired much of its ANCSA entitlement land holdings, the intertwined and adjoining nature of its lands with Federal conservation unit lands is not atypical. In fact, intertwined, adjoining, isolated by, and in-holding are the descriptors of many ANCSA corporation- and State-owned tracts in Alaska, particularly if you consider the practical impacts of such geographic features as mountain ranges, glaciers and large bodies of water. Within the system created by these realities, land management challenges are inevitable between the USFWS in its administration of its conservation units and the rest of us. But that relationship has become more and more strained and complicated by management practices, rules and standards now required by the USFWS in the administration of its refuge system in Alaska.

Unfortunately, the land management philosophy of the USFWS and other Federal land managers in Alaska appears to be evolving away from the underlying principles and compromises of ANCSA and ANILCA that created the refuges and other conservation areas. I will describe for you, as best I can, some of my recent experiences in this area.

44

The current apparent land management philosophy of the USFWS in Alaska as it relates to oil and gas exploration and development on or adjacent to the refuge system can be summed up as: "No. Not here. Not now." Unfortunately, this mantra is inconsistent with the careful compromise that was historically made in order to achieve a satisfactory, if not ideal, land ownership outcome between the competing interests of the Federal Government, the State government and the Alaska Native people. This grand historic compromise led to the creation of a relatively complicated land ownership pattern that includes the so-called "the checker board" pattern, subsurface-only holdings and other extensive "inholdings" within the newly created National Wildlife Refuge system of Alaska in the early 1980s.

Some 35 years later, the relationship between the ANCSA corporations and the State of Alaska, on the one hand, and the USFWS on the other, appears to be diverging. While the ANCSA corporations and the State of Alaska are intent on pursuing oil and gas exploration and development on their lands, as was promised by the grand compromise and the individual compromises that led up to the ANILCA-created refuge system, the USFWS seems intent on finding new ways to say "no" to that activity.

To be clear, the refuge managers usually do not say "no" directly when addressing issues of access to or across their refuges for oil and gas exploration and development or other activity by ANCSA Regional Corporations or other landowners with inholdings or subsurface interests. For most actions for which they are approached, they know that they may not directly and explicitly say "no". They have instead adopted more sophisticated ways to attempt to prevent otherwise authorized activity.

A good example comes from the relatively recent drilling of the Shadura Number 1 exploration well in the Kenai National Wildlife Refuge in the winter of 2010–2011. The Shadura Number 1 was an exploration well drilled by NordAq Energy, Inc., a small independent, on a CIRI oil and gas lease. The Shadura prospect lies in the northern Kenai Peninsula north of Kenai on CIRI-owned subsurface below USFWS surface estate within the KNWR. The Shadura prospect was identified from reprocessing of historical seismic data gathered in a large exploration program by ARCO in the early 1980s under an exploration license from CIRI.

In planning for the exploration well, it became clear to NordAq that the KNWR management greatly preferred an ice road/ice pad exploration program as opposed to a more traditional gravel road to and gravel drilling pad at the exploration site. NordAq therefore planned and began permitting for an ice road/ice pad exploration program. Tailoring its exploration program to an ice road/ice pad-designed program constituted a significant accommodation by NordAq to a minimum impacts approach.

Ice roads and ice pads for oil and gas exploration are common in Alaska. But they are less common in the Cook Inlet basin where the Shadura prospect is located because of the relatively shorter and less predictable winter conditions necessary for the road construction, drilling and testing program, and demobilization necessary to successfully accomplish an oil and gas exploration well. A full exploration drilling program can easily run 75 to 90 days in length, which can be a gamble in the climate of southcentral Alaska and its maritime-influenced environment. For obvious reasons, an ice road/ice pad program requires sustained sub-freezing temperatures for construction and maintenance of the road and pad. Nevertheless, NordAq planned for an ice road/ice pad program during the fall and early winter of 2010.

But as NordAq's field program drew near, the requirements imposed on its ice road/ice pad program shifted. The common means of constructing an ice road is to permit a variety of local freshwater sources for temporary withdrawal to create the construction materials, namely—water to freeze into ice chips to create a road base. The USFWS had other ideas. They would not permit any local freshwater locations within the KNWR for NordAq's ice road. Nor would they permit the scavenging of naturally produced ice from the surface of local lakes or ponds. This leads to the inevitable question, how does one build an ice road if access to freshwater resources is not allowed?

Fortunately, NordAq and its ice road contractor, Peak Oilfield Services Company, were not easily defeated. NordAq and Peak contracted with one of the fish processing plants in Kenai that was closed for the winter to purchase an industrial quantity of ice chips made in its ice makers—normally used to pack and process fresh fish. Peak then trucked the man-made, purchased ice in dump trucks 14 miles, one way to the job site. Even this was not without its challenges as USFWS staff raised questions about whether the water created when the "imported" ice chips melted would change the water chemistry or have any other deleterious effects.

Obviously it seems inherently unfair to require a company to perform its exploration program from an ice road/ice pad system and then subsequently deny access to the local freshwater resources necessary to reasonably construct that ice road/ice pad. It is over-the-top to then question the impact of "imported" ice chips that must be used in lieu of what should be locally sourced ice. But that is exactly what happened to NordAq at its Shadura project in 2010 and 2011. These are the sorts of inconsistencies that are now common behaviors by the USFWS in dealing with oil and gas operators working on CIRI's KNWR lands.

NordAq persevered and prevailed to successfully drill an apparent discovery well with its Shadura Number 1 well in February 2011, some 3 years ago, but it has not quite been able to get back to the discovery location to drill a confirmation well and begin production in earnest. That is a story that will continue below.

JUNK SCIENCE OR LACK OF SCIENCE

Land management of oil and gas activity should be premised on sound science but recent Federal actions in Alaska highlight decisions premised on junk science or a lack of science. Many of these actions do not emanate from the USFWS but the impacts have an interplay with activities on or near refuges. The principal action of this nature is the designation of geographically massive critical habitat areas for endangered species.

The two species of note in this regard are the polar bear and the Cook Inlet beluga whale. Although the designation of the polar bear as endangered and its subsequent critical habitat area do not directly affect CIRI's KNWR interests, I mention it here as an analogue because of the scale, scope and practical impact on oil and gas activities on the North Slope of Alaska. I will focus instead on the designation of and critical habitat area of the Cook Inlet beluga whale.

The Cook Inlet beluga whale was designated as an endangered subspecies of the beluga whale, which is not endangered. Due to a variety of unique features of the Cook Inlet beluga whale and its habitat, very little scientific data and analysis exists about the whale, its seasonal migration and local habitat areas. The Cook Inlet beluga whale is even a species without an accurate population count or model, although this aspect has been greatly improved in the past several years, in large part due to data gathered by private companies doing work in the upper Cook Inlet. Unfortunately, little accurate counting and population modeling was performed prior to a noticeable decline in the whales' numbers in the last two decades. Thus, great uncertainty surrounds even the baseline question of what a healthy population number is for this particular whale subspecies. Nevertheless, the National Marine Fisheries Service ("NMFS") designated the Cook Inlet beluga whale as an endangered species—almost certainly a justified action. But what it did next was less justified. When designating the critical habitat area the NMFS seemingly just took a Sharpie to the map and drew a line across Cook Inlet in two places from east to west. NMFS then declared all of Cook Inlet, including all of Turnagain Arm and Knik Arm, including intertidal estuaries, river and creek mouths, tidal mudflats and all other areas up to the mean high tide mark, to be class one critical habitat. Between the second line and the first was declared class two critical habitat. This is a massive geographical area with an enormous length of coastline—an area I often equate to the Gulf Coast for all of Texas starting at the Mexican border and running up into or beyond Louisiana. This is a massive withdrawal of water and adjoining tidelands for critical habitat, particularly without any underlying science to justify its designation as "critical" habitat.

There are direct carry over effects of the Cook Inlet beluga whale critical habitat area designation on oil and gas activities in the KNWR. At this point, I have only witnessed one impact but another is equally predictable and inevitable. The first is negative impact on seismic operations necessary to properly image CIRI's subsurface estate within the KNWR to identify good exploration targets for oil and gas. CIRI has licensed a large part of its Cook Inlet lands to Apache Alaska under an exploration agreement. Apache Alaska spent several years attempting to permit what would have been the largest 3d seismic program in the history of Alaska. This program was intended to shoot modern, 3d seismic in a continuous and robust program from offshore, through the transition zone of the tidelands and onto the uplands, including CIRI's KNWR subsurface holdings. Due to an inability of the various Federal agencies to coordinate their individual permitting activities for Apache Alaska's proposed program and timely issue permits, a process greatly complicated by the Cook Inlet beluga whale critical habitat area, Apache Alaska abandoned its 3d program and replaced it with a much smaller, discontinuous 2d seismic program. Thus, a scientifically unsupported critical habitat designation impaired CIRI's ability to have an oil and gas lessee properly image its subsurface resource lands in the KNWR.

Unfortunately CIRI's experience with Federal actions based on a lack of science is not its only experience of late. We have also seen issues raised by USFWS junk science. Going back to NordAq's Shadura discovery story, the USFWS also impeded its progress toward a reasonably timely development, in part by employing junk science within the permitting process for a right-of-way application. NordAq toiled for more than 30 months after its Shadura discovery to achieve the development permits necessary to construct a simple, single land gravel road and pad that is necessary to further develop the field. This permitting process took so long because the USFWS insisted that a full environmental impact statement process was required even though the activity is simple, low-impact and cannot be denied. In the process, the USFWS raised a habitat issue of note: peat pipes.

We were shocked to discover the issue of peat pipes raised in the Shadura development EIS process. The reason we were so surprised is because none of us had ever even heard of such a thing as a peat pipe. Our astonishment was well founded. As far as I know, a peat pipe has never been identified anywhere in North America.

A peat pipe is a near-surface, subsurface hydrological feature of the extensive, continuous and relatively homogenous peat bogs of northern England. It is a natural channel, or pipe, that is eroded into the surrounding peat over time by the movement of subsurface water. Peat pipes are shallow and somewhat ephemeral features that often link surface streams and ponds with the shallow subsurface hydrological features.

Despite no identified peat pipes in the Kenai Peninsula or southcentral Alaska, and no credible evidence that would indicate that any peat pipes exist in the KNWR, peat pipes were an issue that had to be addressed in the Shadura development EIS process. The peat pipes issue highlights the consequences of junk science as applied by the USFWS to oil and gas activities within the refuge system in Alaska—NordAq's permitting process was slowed and made substantially more expensive by addressing an imaginary issue.

INADEQUATE STAFFING AND CHANGING RULES

Two practical realities dominate the interaction between oil and gas operators and the USFWS: inadequate staffing and changing rules. The USFWS is faced with too few technical experts to properly and timely process oil and gas activities on or crossing its refuge lands and many of those tasked with such activities do so without adequate technical education or training in oil and gas specific issues.

The practical impact of too few oil and gas technical experts within the USFWS has the predictable consequence of slowing down all permitting and oversight activities. But there is also a lack of oil and gas specific expertise, which has an additional consequence of permitters focusing on the wrong issues or creating imaginary issues.

The very changes being contemplated by the USFWS right now highlights the other practical problem: constantly shifting rules. I have heard numerous times from my lessees about the problem of moving goalposts.

Another example from the NordAq Shadura case study highlights this issue. As mentioned above, NordAq's Shadura development requires an access road to get back to the Shadura prospect, which is not accessible by existing roads. The Shadura access road was designed as a single-lane gravel road in order to minimize the impact on the KNWR and its surface habitat. To make the single lane design safe and serviceable, it was designed with turnouts every quarter mile to facilitate bi-directional traffic. This design was incorporated into the right-of-way design that went through the EIS evaluation process. Except after the final EIS was issued the USFWS attempted to renegotiate the design of the road to eliminate turnouts, in an apparent attempt to further limit the habitat impact of the Shadura road. Such an after-the-process attempt to change the road was a classic example of constantly changing rules and expectations from the USFWS staff. Operators are happy to comply with reasonable rules, but they need to know what the rules are—and the rules need to stay constant.

THE DE FACTO NATIONAL PARK SERVICE MANAGEMENT REGIME

Perhaps the explanation for the USFWS's recent behaviors lies in an underlying seismic shift in management philosophies by Federal land management agencies with regard to their lands in Alaska. The USFWS and other Federal land managers—such as the Forest Service and the Bureau of Land Management—in Alaska appear to be adopting a de facto National Park Service (''NPS'') management regime. Many of the proposed rulemakings recently have either implicitly or explicitly been premised on, refer to, or adopt standards similar to those of the NPS. In fact, the recent proposed rulemaking by the USFWS explicitly referenced the oil and gas rules and standards of the NPS as both guidance and inspiration. Using the NPS system is inappropriate.

The problem inherent in this shift is that the NPS manages for one explicit purpose, to preserve the wild, natural and undeveloped character of its lands, with a minimal accommodation to humans for the sole, express purpose of authorized and limited visitation of the otherwise undisturbed natural environment. But other Federal lands are not parks and, accordingly, those lands should not be managed as such. The National Wildlife Refuge System in Alaska, and elsewhere, has different purposes. And, importantly, the individual lands that comprise National Wildlife Refuges often have a much different and more complicated history than those within the National Park System.

In many, and perhaps most, cases in Alaska, the National Wildlife Refuge system was created with a mix of inholdings and subsurface interests included within the exterior boundaries of individual refuges in order to maximize the geographic area encompassed by that refuge. By 1980 when most of the National Wildlife Refuges in Alaska were created, there were already many competing applications for the same and adjoining lands that were due to the then-new ANCSA corporations and to the State of Alaska. Many of these lands were under competing selection by these non-Federal entities. In order to carve out these very large National Wildlife Refuge areas, compromises were struck with the non-Federal entities. Thus, in creating the refuges in this manner, the rights of others were necessarily stirred into the dough of the refuge system in Alaska. It is now impossible to cleanly or fairly extract those interests some 30 to 40 years after the loaf was baked. Attempting to recreate the refuges as parks does not work in Alaska.

THE ALASKA PARADOX

I must mention one final overarching theme. Alaska is a special place, no question about it. It is beautiful, enormous and largely undeveloped: a national treasure. Alaska also holds a national treasure's worth of developed and undeveloped resources. And therein lies a set of circumstances that give rise to what I like to call "the Alaska Paradox."

The Alaska Paradox results from the convergence of two powerful and competing realities in resource development in a place like Alaska. There is an economic reality that drives the scale of resource developments in Alaska to the very large or world class in scale. This enormous project scale is necessary to justify and fund the development and permitting risk of a new resources project in a place as big, as Arctic and as undeveloped as Alaska. Where oil and gas operators in the Lower 48 may target prospective resources in the hundreds of thousands of barrels of oil equivalent, in Alaska they typically target minimums in the tens of millions of barrels—and even more if the prospect location is far from infrastructure in an undeveloped area.

The competing reality is that world class-scale projects in an otherwise undeveloped area create significant new impacts that in turn engender enormous scrutiny.

Let me give you an example: the Red Dog Mine. The Red Dog Mine is one of the world's largest zinc deposits. It sits some 90 miles from Kotzebue, the only community of any scale within the Northwest Arctic Borough, an area the geographic equivalent of the State of Indiana with a mere 7,200 residents, fully half or more of which live in Kotzebue. The Red Dog Mine required the development and construction of its own access road, port, airport, camp and housing facilities, and power plant in addition to the ordinary mine and mine support facilities—all in an extremely remote, extremely arctic and completely undeveloped area of Alaska. Although the mine was and is extremely successful and has had an extraordinary environmental record, and its development and operation singularly supports the finances of the Northwest Arctic Borough and its communities, it is not clear to me that the Red Dog Mine could be developed today. It is simply too large and it and its attendant infrastructure have too much of an impact on the otherwise undeveloped environment around it. This is the reality of the Alaska Paradox: projects must be very large, but very large projects engender significant and sustained opposition and scrutiny.

NEW RULES ARE NEITHER AUTHORIZED NOR NEEDED

The USFWS has recently proposed a set of new rules to govern oil and gas exploration, development and production on the national wildlife refuge system. These rules are neither authorized nor needed in Alaska.

The proposed rules would disturb the careful statutory balance between the ANCSA corporations, and specifically CIRI, and the State of Alaska on one hand, and the Federal interests on the other. Accordingly, the proposed rules may not be implemented. Many of the proposed rules, e.g. bonding requirements, tread on the prerogative of the lessor and royalty owner and are not an appropriate action by the USFWS. Such requirements would impose an additional and unnecessary financial burden on oil and gas operators. The USFWS's proposed actions would constitute a usurping of the authority and responsibility of the landowner/lessor and are inappropriate. The proposed rules would also constitute a unilateral rewriting of the statutorily crafted rights and duties some 30 to 40 years after many of these issues were settled. The USFWS is not authorized to upset this congressionally crafted balance.

CONCLUSION

I can think of no circumstances under which the U.S. Fish and Wildlife Service's proposed new oil and gas rules are needed or would be justified in their application in Alaska. The effort to rewrite these rules is at best an attempt to usurp the role of the oil and gas lessor of inholdings, adjoining tracts or subsurface oil and gas rights below Alaska refuges. It is at worst an attempt to unilaterally rewrite the terms of a carefully crafted compromise between the Alaska Native Corporations and the State of Alaska, on the one hand, and the Federal Government on the other.

———

Dr. FLEMING. Thank you, Mr. Schutt.

Mr. Matson, you are now recognized for 5 minutes to present testimony on behalf of the Defenders of Wildlife.

STATEMENT OF NOAH MATSON, VICE PRESIDENT, DEFENDERS OF WILDLIFE

Mr. MATSON. Thank you, Mr. Chairman, and members of the subcommittee. My name is Noah Matson, I am the Vice President of Landscape Conservation for Defenders of Wildlife. And thank you for the opportunity to provide input on this important issue.

It has come up a bunch of times, where these regulations, this idea for regulations, come from. The Government Accountability Office, period. It appeared in their 2003 report and again in their 2007 report. And they specifically believe that the Fish and Wildlife Service has the authority to do this, and they recommended that they do actually go ahead and implement better regulations. And I will hopefully explain why.

And, finally, the Fish and Wildlife Service is not proposing to deny access to anybody. They are proposing to restore a proper balance between resource protection and the development of private mineral interests.

I have been involved in this issue for almost 15 years. In 2000 I sent one of my staff to a number of national wildlife refuges in Louisiana to help Defenders of Wildlife better understand how and why oil and gas development occurs on national wildlife refuges, and what the impacts of that development are. What my staff discovered was nothing short of shocking, and I have personally been to a number of refuges since, and witnessed the impacts myself.

I have prepared a slideshow of a number of these photographs from our visit to these refuges in Louisiana, as well as more recent images. As my staff toured these refuges with the Fish and Wildlife Service staff, they discovered a brine spill near a well that refuge staff previously was not aware of. Slide.

[Slide]

Mr. MATSON. My staff came back with pictures of 55-gallon drums oozing with black chemicals, open waste ponds topped with sheens of oil. Slide.

[Slide]

Mr. MATSON. Abandoned, rusting storage tanks. Slide.

[Slide]

Mr. MATSON. A rusted pipe leaking into a refuge mark. You can see the sheen right there.

But that was a long time ago. Surely, surely, over the last 14 years, after three separate Government Accountability Office reports, things would be different today. Slide, please.

[Slide]

Mr. MATSON. They are not. This photo of 55-gallon drums and 5-gallon pails strewn about a refuge with unknown contents was taken just in March of this year, 2 months ago. Slide.

[Slide]

Mr. MATSON. This photo of the high-quality repair jobs that we are seeing at national wildlife refuges was taken just in February. Slide.

[Slide]

Mr. MATSON. And one of my favorites, a leaking tank repaired with duct tape and a garbage bag was taken on a refuge in March of this year.

On many national wildlife refuges, development of privately owned oil and gas minerals recounts the Wild West. The existing single paragraph of Fish and Wildlife Service regulations pertaining to non-Federal mineral rights on national wildlife refuges is completely inadequate. It is so full of qualifiers and discretion that it is meaningless as a practical tool for managing oil and gas exploration and development.

In short, the current regulations cannot be relied on to protect the wildlife values of affected wildlife refuges, nor the health, safety, and enjoyment of the visiting public.

Oil and gas exploration and development is extensive, and is damaging refuge resources. At St. Catherine Creek National Wildlife Refuge in Mississippi, oil and brine spills have led to significant soil and vegetation damage on the refuge. Slide, please.

[Slide]

Mr. MATSON. The legacy of brine spills is evident in this picture. The field you are looking at should be a woodland. But after a brine spill years ago, nothing grew on this plot except salt-tolerant shrubs.

And just last month the Service staff at the Catahoula National Wildlife Refuge in Louisiana discovered numerous spills and leaks at an oil production facility on the refuge. The Service is still assessing the extent and scope of that damage.

Unfortunately, taxpayers are being left with the cleanup bill. There are at least 3,300 inactive wells on national wildlife refuges. The Fish and Wildlife Service does not have adequate assurances that the responsible party will properly plug the wells and reclaim the sites. The cost of plugging wells and restoring habitat is significant.

For example, the Lower Rio Grande National Valley National Wildlife Refuge in Texas cleanup and restoration costs for just

50

three wells in 2011 was $1.2 million, or $400,000 per well. And at St. Catherine Creek National Wildlife Refuge in Mississippi, re-plugging an abandoned well and restoring the costs, cost the tax-payers $260,000. These costs should be borne by the private mineral owners and operators.

Slide, please.

[Slide]

Mr. Matson. The Fish and Wildlife Service's current grossly in-adequate regulations and capacity will not prevent these costs from being borne by taxpayers, nor do they allow the Service to properly manage the surface activities of non-Federal oil and gas develop-ment.

You know, basic information procedures like bonding, special use permits, requiring proof of ownership, are not currently required. The qualifiers and absence of any procedural requirements in the Fish and Wildlife Service's existing regulation render them vir-tually meaningless, and stand in sharp contrast to the National Park Service's comprehensive and reasonable oversight to the same category of activities. The Refuge System deserves nothing less. Thank you.

[The prepared statement of Mr. Matson follows:]

PREPARED STATEMENT OF NOAH MATSON, VICE PRESIDENT FOR LANDSCAPE CONSERVATION AND CLIMATE ADAPTATION, DEFENDERS OF WILDLIFE

Mr. Chairman and members of the subcommittee, my name is Noah Matson and I am the Vice President for Landscape Conservation and Climate Adaptation for Defenders of Wildlife. Thank you for the opportunity to provide input to the sub-committee on ''Oil and Gas Activities within Our Nation's Wildlife Refuge System.'' This is an extremely important issue facing the National Wildlife Refuge System and the incredible wildlife the Refuge System was established to protect and I ap-preciate the subcommittee's interest in the issue.

I have been following this issue for almost 15 years. In 2000 I sent one of my staff to a number of national wildlife refuges in Louisiana to help Defenders of Wildlife better understand how and why oil and gas development occurs on national wildlife refuges and what the impacts of that development are. What my staff dis-covered was nothing short of shocking.

I have included a number of photographs from our visit to these refuges in Louisiana. As my staff toured these refuges with Fish and Wildlife Service staff, they discovered a brine spill near a well that refuge staff previously was not aware of. My staff came back with pictures of 55 gallon drums oozing black toxic chemi-cals; open waste ponds topped with sheens of oil; abandoned, rusting storage tanks; and rusted pipes and well heads that provided no confidence they would not leak in the future.

On many national wildlife refuges development of privately owned oil and gas minerals recounts the ''Wild West.'' The existing single paragraph of Fish and Wildlife Service regulations pertaining to private mineral rights on national wildlife refuges is so full of qualifiers and discretion that it is completely inadequate for the Service to be able to reasonably manage surface activities connected with oil and gas exploration and development in order to protect the fish and wildlife values of affected wildlife refuges, Federal trust resources, Federal property, and the health, safety and enjoyment of the visiting public.

OIL AND GAS EXPLORATION AND DEVELOPMENT IS EXTENSIVE AND IS DAMAGING REFUGE RESOURCES

According to the Fish and Wildlife Service, over 200 national wildlife refuges have existing oil and gas infrastructure including 103 refuges and 4 wetland management districts that have active oil and gas wells. In total there are more than 5,000 wells with almost 1,700 of those wells actively producing oil and gas. I consider these minimum figures. From my experience, and confirmed by the Government Account-ability Office (GAO), the Fish and Wildlife Service does not have an adequate sys-tem for tracking oil and gas development within wildlife refuges.

St. Catherine Creek National Wildlife Refuge in Mississippi is high on the list of refuges with the most oil and gas wells, with nearly 500, over 60 of which are active. Oil and brine spills have led to significant soil and vegetation damage on the refuge. One such spill occurred in 1993, when a massive leak of briny water, pulled up from oil and gas operations, flooded 21 acres of sensitive coastal habitat. The salt levels left in the soil were high enough to cause acute and chronic effects to tree species and aquatic organisms that persist to this day.

More recently, in 2012, Hagerman National Wildlife Refuge in Texas experienced a leak of oilfield brine into a mature woodlands. The brine spill killed over 80 hardwood trees—two of these trees were estimated to be over 150 years old. The Fish and Wildlife Service estimated it would cost over $150,000 to restore the damaged habitat.

Just last month, the Service staff at the Catahoula National Wildlife Refuge in Louisiana discovered numerous spills and leaks at an oil production facility on the refuge. The Service is still assessing the extent and scope of the damage.

The impacts of oil and gas development are not limited to large spills—even frequent small spills can be deadly over time. According to the Service, a study of Atchafalaya and Delta National Wildlife Refuges in Louisiana found that "levels of oil contamination near oil and gas facilities are lethal to most species of wildlife, even though refuge staff were not aware of any large spills."

Overall, the impacts of oil and gas development on wildlife, ecosystems, and wildlife refuge management are well known and include:

- Destruction, degradation, and fragmentation of wildlife habitat through clearing and construction of wells, well pads, seismic lines, storage tanks and ponds, pipelines and other infrastructure and the movement of heavy drilling equipment across sensitive habitat.
- Leaks and spills of oil, brine, produced water, contaminated drilling muds, and other toxic chemicals that harm wildlife, vegetation, water quality, air quality and human health.
- Introduction of invasive species that compete with native plants, wildlife and habitat.
- Disturbance of wildlife during construction and operation of facilities.
- Conflicts with important wildlife refuge management activities, for example by inhibiting necessary prescribed fire operations near oil and gas facilities.
- Conflicts with other priority forms of public use and enjoyment of refuge resources like wildlife dependent recreational activities.

TAXPAYERS ARE BEING LEFT WITH THE CLEANUP BILL

There at least 3,300 inactive wells on national wildlife refuges. A substantial proportion of those wells are likely abandoned, or will be abandoned, and in many if not most cases, the Fish and Wildlife Service does not have adequate assurances that the responsible party will properly plug the wells and reclaim the sites.

Let's assume conservatively for purposes of discussion that only 1,000 of these inactive wells are abandoned and orphaned—with no known operator. The State of Louisiana requires a $25,000 bond for operators of 1–10 wells. If you assume that it costs just $25,000 to plug and reclaim a single well, then taxpayers could be stuck with a $25 million bill from deadbeat drillers to cover restoration costs. The real experience of the Fish and Wildlife Service, however, suggests the costs of plugging and reclaiming well sites is much, much more.

At the Lower Rio Grande Valley National Wildlife Refuge in Texas, Fish and Wildlife Service staff spent 15 years negotiating with the Texas Railroad Commission, which governs oil and gas activities in the State, about plugging three abandoned wells on the refuge. In 2011 the abandoned well sites were finally cleaned up and equipment were removed from the refuge at the cost of $1.2 million—or $400,000 per well.

At St. Catherine Creek National Wildlife Refuge in Mississippi, refuge staff discovered a leaking oil well in 2012. The well had been improperly plugged and abandoned in 1983. The State's policy transferred responsibility for re-plugging the well site and cleanup to the current surface owner—the Fish and Wildlife Service. The Environmental Protection Agency (EPA) ultimately assumed jurisdiction and all costs of the cleanup because of its size. Re-plugging the well alone cost $95,000 (well above the $10,000 bonding requirements in Mississippi, or the $25,000 bonding requirement in Louisiana for a single well). Site restoration cost an additional $165,000. In total, it cost taxpayers $260,000 to cleanup, plug, and restore a single abandoned well site because of inadequate State and Federal regulations.

As a well declines in productivity it is usually sold, often multiple times, making it difficult to track down responsible parties and enforce cleanup costs. Each subsequent owner is often a lower budget operation that is trying to squeeze the last drops of oil or natural gas at the least cost out of the ground. The last owners often disappear or claim bankruptcy.

The future restoration costs and liabilities of the 5,000 wells on national wildlife refuges will cost hundreds of millions of dollars. These costs should be borne by the private mineral owners and operators. Existing Federal and State regulations are not adequately protecting either irreplaceable national wildlife refuge resources or Federal taxpayers from these liabilities.

EXISTING FEDERAL AND STATE REGULATIONS ARE INADEQUATE

The examples I have provided of past damage to national wildlife refuges from private oil and gas exploration and development, and the lack of adequate financial assurances to properly manage, plug, restore and reclaim well sites once they have been abandoned, clearly demonstrate that the current system of State and Federal oil and gas regulations applicable to national wildlife refuges is not properly protecting the surface resources that belong to the American people. States prioritize well site inspections, enforcement, and reclamation dollars to State and private surface lands above areas owned or managed by the Federal Government. And even if they could be expeditiously tapped, State bonds for oil and gas development do not adequately cover the full cost of plugging abandoned wells, pulling pipelines, storage tanks and other infrastructure, and restoring sites to natural habitat.

As of 2011, the Texas Railroad Commission had only 153 inspectors to monitor 263,233 producing oil and gas wells. In order to visit each well once per year, each inspector would have to visit seven wells a day—a near impossible task given travel times, necessary follow up on violations and a myriad of other factors. And visiting a well once a year is hardly adequate to ensure compliance with State standards. Other States have fewer inspectors per well. Relying on States to protect the property and wildlife interests of the Federal Government and the American taxpayer within national wildlife refuges simply will not work.

Similarly, the Fish and Wildlife Service's current grossly inadequate regulations, procedures, and capacity are not up to the task as well. For example, Upper Ouachita National Wildlife Refuge in Louisiana has over 1,000 wells—more than any other national wildlife refuge. Yet the refuge has no dedicated staff to manage that development, does not know the full extent of mineral rights owners, and does not require special use permits or operators to post a bond.

Basic information and procedures like this are not only essential to provide balanced and reasonable protection for the wildlife and recreational values that our national wildlife refuges provide, but they are customary on other land ownerships. Unfortunately, the Service has acted for far too long as if it has had no authority whatsoever to impose even minimal reasonable restrictions on private mineral development that are necessary to reduce serious harm to refuge resources. This is simply wrong, and we commend the Fish and Wildlife Service for finally recognizing they in fact have the authority and are willing to develop a thoughtful and comprehensive approach to protect the resources they were charged with protecting, while providing reasonable access to private mineral rights.

The Fish and Wildlife Service's single paragraph in the Code of Federal Regulations (50 CFR § 29.32) regarding non-Federal oil and gas development reads as follows (emphasis added):

> Persons holding mineral rights in wildlife refuge lands by reservation in the conveyance to the United States and persons holding mineral rights in such lands which rights vested prior to the acquisition of the lands by the United States shall, *to the greatest extent practicable*, conduct all exploration, development, and production operations in such a manner as to prevent damage, erosion, pollution, or contamination to the lands, waters, facilities and vegetation of the area. *So far as is practicable*, such operations must also be conducted without interference with the operation of the refuge or disturbance to the wildlife thereon. Physical occupancy of the area *must be kept to the minimum space compatible with the conduct of efficient mineral operations*. Persons conducting mineral operations on refuge areas must comply with all applicable Federal and State laws and regulations for the protection of wildlife and the administration of the area. Oil field brine, slag, and all other waste and contaminating substances *must be kept in the smallest practicable area*, must be confined so as to prevent escape as a result of rains and high water or otherwise, and *must be removed from the area as quickly as practicable* in such a manner as to prevent contamination, pollution, damage, or injury to the lands, waters, facilities, or vegetation of the refuge or to wildlife. Structures and equipment must be removed from the

area when the need for them has ended. Upon the cessation of operations *the area shall be restored as nearly as possible* to its condition prior to the commencement of operations. Nothing in this section shall be applied so as to contravene or nullify rights vested in holders of mineral interests on refuge lands.

The qualifiers, lack of definition, and absence of any procedural requirements in this regulation render them virtually meaningless and stand in sharp contrast to the National Park Service's (NPS) comprehensive and substantive oversight of the same category of activities. Promulgated in 1979, and currently being updated, NPS's rules at 36 CFR § 9.30 establish a detailed and precautionary approach to the approval and subsequent management of non-Federal oil and gas operations on NPS lands. At the core of this program is the requirement that oil and gas operators submit a detailed plan of operations, with precise information concerning the location, extent, and duration of proposed activities and associated infrastructure; the affected environment and anticipated environmental consequences; technologically achievable alternatives to the proposed operations; measures to protect surface and subsurface waters; and many other standards. NPS also retains the authority to reject inadequate or incomplete plans of operations.

Additionally, NPS's regulations require specific authorization for any use of water within NPS lands, establish substantive reclamation requirements and operating standards, mandate registration of oil and gas related commercial vehicles with the agency, require guaranteed performance bonds, provide for specific damage clauses, and allow public participation and comment on a proposed plan of operations.

The courts have upheld the Park Service's approach. According to the GAO:

> *In Dunn McCampbell Royalty Interest, Inc.* v. *National Park Service*, 964 F. Supp. 1125 (S.D. Tex. 1995), *aff'd on other grounds*, 112 F.3d 1283 (5th Cir. 1997), the court ruled that the National Park Service has authority to reasonably regulate private owners' access to their oil and gas interests located beneath park system lands, by requiring approval of a plan of operations before commencement of exploration or production activities. The court relied on language in the National Park Service Organic Act directing the Park Service to ''protect and regulate'' national parks so as to ''conserve the scenery and the natural and historic objects and the wildlife therein and to provide for the enjoyment of the same in such manner and by such means as will leave them unimpaired for the enjoyment of future generations,'' as well as language directing the Department of the Interior to issue regulations ''as . . . deem[ed] necessary or proper for the use of the parks . . . under the jurisdiction of the National Park Service.''

The Refuge System similarly has a strong organic act, the National Wildlife Refuge System Improvement Act (16 U.S.C. 668dd–668ee) that declares that the mission of the Refuge System is to ''administer a national network of lands and waters for the conservation, management, and where appropriate, restoration of the fish, wildlife, and plant resources and their habitats within the United States for the benefit of present and future generations of Americans.'' The Refuge Improvement Act directs the Secretary of the Interior to ''ensure that the biological integrity, diversity and environmental health of the System are maintained,'' and authorizes the Service to issue regulations to carry out the Act.

Though a more thorough legal analysis during the rulemaking process would be helpful, the Fish and Wildlife Service clearly has the authority to establish reasonable regulations to protect Federal property and to achieve its wildlife conservation mission.

THE FISH AND WILDLIFE SERVICE IS COMPELLED TO IMPROVE REGULATIONS PERTAINING TO THE SURFACE DEVELOPMENT OF NON-FEDERAL MINERAL RIGHTS UNDERNEATH NATIONAL WILDLIFE REFUGES

The Government Accountability Office has studied the problems surrounding the exploration and development of non-Federal oil and gas on national wildlife refuges fully three times since 2001 and has provided a compelling basis for the Fish and Wildlife Service to enact changes to its regulatory structure. A third of all national wildlife refuges have some form of oil and gas development occurring within their boundaries, the vast majority of which involve the development of private oil and gas interests. That development regularly causes harm to wildlife, habitat, water and air quality, other priority public use and enjoyment of wildlife refuges, and interferes with important refuge management priorities. Existing State and Fish and Wildlife Service regulations, controls, and capacity are grossly inadequate for properly protecting important and irreplaceable wildlife refuge resources. Based on

these facts, the Fish and Wildlife Service, in order to meet the conservation mandates established by Congress in managing the National Wildlife Refuge System,
desperately needs to update and expand its regulations to reasonably manage and
provide a nationally consistent approach to the development of non-Federal oil and
gas resources within the boundaries of national wildlife refuges.

Defenders of Wildlife looks forward to working with the Fish and Wildlife Service
to ensure reasonable and balanced regulations are enacted.

**Attachment – Photographs from National Wildlife Refuges with non-federal oil and gas
development**

A typical well pad results in acres of direct habitat
loss that cannot support wildlife. This habitat is
likely never to be reclaimed.

Atchafalya National Wildlife Refuge, Louisiana

A tank battery reflected in spilled oil.

Catahoula National Wildlife Refuge, Louisiana

Pipe slowly leaking oil, destroying surrounding
wetlands. Old, rusting, leaking pipes plague refuges
in Louisiana.

Atchafalya National Wildlife Refuge, Louisiana

An old storage tank with rusty holes, covered with duct tape, discarded and left on site at one of the well head sites. Clean-up of abandoned sites is almost unheard of on Louisiana refuges.

Atchafalya National Wildlife Refuge, Louisiana

Discarded 55-gallon drum oozing oil, open waste or containment pond, and large-scale development.

Catahoula National Wildlife Refuge, Louisiana

ADDITIONAL TESTIMONY OF NOAH MATSON, DEFENDERS OF WILDLIFE

Chairman Fleming, Ranking Member Sablan, and members of the subcommittee, thank you again for inviting me to testify before the subcommittee. I am providing additional material relevant to the hearing.

The subject of oil and gas development on the Kenai National Wildlife Refuge in Alaska was a point of discussion during the hearing. Federal minerals were leased on the Kenai refuge before the 1966 National Wildlife Refuge System Improvement Act. No additional Federal minerals have ever been offered, and in fact, additional leasing has been officially determined to be ''incompatible'' with the wildlife conservation purposes of the refuge.

It is important to point out that this existing development has caused substantial harm to the refuge. Attached to this letter I am including a report produced by Defenders of Wildlife and Audubon documenting the numerous spills and explosions that have released toxic chemicals on the refuge. The refuge documented the presence of deformed frogs, among other impacts.

I bring this to your attentions to demonstrate that reasonable regulations of non-Federal mineral development are sorely needed to prevent similar problems in the future if and when those resources are developed.

Thank you.

Attachment

REPORT ON TOXIC TUNDRA BY DEFENDERS OF WILDLIFE AND AUDUBON

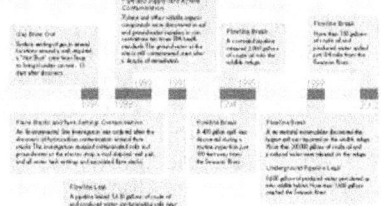

Groundwater in some areas of the wildlife refuge shows contamination at 10 times the legal limit established by the Environmental Protection Agency.

Major Spills Within the Swanson River Oil Field on Kenai Refuge

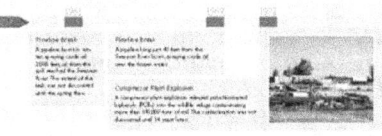

Spilled Oil and Other Contaminants Threaten Birds and Other Wildlife

Crippling Frog Deformities Found in Oil Fields Within the Kenai Refuge Warrant Further Investigation

Further Investigation is Needed to Determine the Full Extent of the Toxic Legacy on Kenai National Wildlife Refuge

Don't Repeat the Kenai Mistake — Keep Oil Drilling, Oil Spills and Industrial Infrastructure Out of the Pristine Arctic Refuge

FPO needs to be scanned

Dr. FLEMING. OK. Mr. Matson concludes his testimony. At this point we will begin Member questioning for the witnesses. To allow all Members to participate, and to ensure we can hear from all of our witnesses today, Members are limited to 5 minutes for their questions. However, if Members have additional questions, we can have more than one round of questions.

Here we go. Just kind of an opening comment from some of the statements made in the testimony I would certainly want to address here. For instance, Mr. Naatz talks about a solution looking for a problem. I agree. This sounds to me like—the way I would put it is a hammer looking for a nail. We have so many problems that we need to deal with in this Nation, and we have States taking care of problems here. It makes no sense to go looking for more problems, particularly in a time of austerity that we are here today.

Of course, Mr. Matson shows us some pictures today. We have no idea whether those are contrived, we have had no ability to evaluate those situations. You heard earlier from testimony of a gentleman showing the damage done, again, barrels just like that were shown there, that was done by BLM in Alaska. So, again, I would just sum that up by saying that Mr. Guertin reassured us there has never been a major spill in a refuge area. I think that is testimony for a lot of things here today.

Now, Mr. Naatz, Mr. Powell, Mr. Schutt, you can kind of take these as you want. Is there any doubt in your mind that State regulations are committed to protecting human health, groundwater, surface water, and public safety at these refuge sites?

Mr. NAATZ. Mr. Chairman, I will start. I can tell you from IPAA's standpoint, we have great confidence in the State regulatory agencies. Again, the States know—and I referenced in my testimony the kind of diverse nature of where oil and gas activity happens, all the way from Alaska to your State, Louisiana, Colorado—the States know the hydrology, the States know the geology, the States know how to get that done. And, again, we have strong confidence in the ability of the States to regulate the oil and gas activities.

Mr. POWELL. Well, I will defer to the IPAA, who has more experience with the field operations. But in NARO's opinion, the State regulations have been more than sufficient, and do not feel that further regulation is warranted.

Dr. FLEMING. OK. Mr. Schutt?

Mr. SCHUTT. I would agree with the prior two speakers, the State system in Alaska is more than adequate to protect health, safety, human interests, and the environment. I would add that the Fish and Wildlife Service in the one refuge where it does have active oil and gas operations, the Kenai, with regard to my lessees, does do active regulation of those lessees in many of the same ways it proposes to do so in the notice of proposed rulemaking. They require a special use permit, they require proof of ownership, running back to CIRI's subsurface, the require reclamation bond for any surface infrastructure.

Dr. FLEMING. So——

Mr. POWELL. They are actively regulating my lessees, as we sit here today.

Dr. FLEMING. Yes. Thank you for that. Again, basically, what we are saying here is the expertise and the experience lies with the States. States have been doing this for many years, and doing a very good job.

Are there certain States whose regulations need to be improved, or major gaps that need to be closed?

Mr. NAATZ. Mr. Chairman, IPAA is a Federal trade—we really haven't looked at that. You know, we would defer to the States. The only thing I would add further to the—to your—to the comments before, is this idea that we run into all the time, that the States don't do a good job of regulating.

Again, when you are in State capitals, when you are dealing with State regulatory agencies, it is far easier to get changes. If there are problems that need to be changed, the States can do that. So, again, I wouldn't—I don't have the expertise to know specific States, but the ability to address problems——

Dr. FLEMING. Right.

Mr. NAATZ [continuing]. Is far easier done at the State capital than here, in Washington.

Dr. FLEMING. Right, far more nimble, far more responsive, absolutely. And what about Louisiana?

Mr. POWELL. I am not a complete expert on the regulations in Louisiana. However, it is my understanding that we have sufficient regulations, if not more than enough, that support their operations. For this reason, I would rather have it in the hands of Louisiana, rather than blanket regulations across the United States by the Service.

Dr. FLEMING. Well, to sum a recent conversation we had with Fishery and Wildlife is that Louisiana is one of the best States when it comes to regulations. Apparently, they treat wells, oil and gas activity on refuge land, no differently than they do private land. It is all the same to them. And in spite of what photographs may have been shown today, Louisiana does it right, and we get that straight from Fisheries and Wildlife.

With that, I yield to the Ranking Member for 5 minutes for questioning.

Mr. SABLAN. Well, thank you very much, Mr. Chairman. Let me start with a yes or no with each one of you.

I am new here, so—but let me ask. Do we understand that your testimony here is under oath?

Mr. NAATZ. Yes.

Mr. POWELL. Yes.

Mr. SCHUTT. Yes.

Mr. MATSON. Yes.

Mr. SABLAN. All right. So let me go to my other question. I mean, in all cases, wells and infrastructure are abandoned due to inadequate finances of an operator, in many cases. So these costs are passed on to the taxpayers. Do you believe the taxpayers should incur the costs associated with damage to refuge resources from leaks and spills, inadequate plumbing, abandonment, and reclamation? Sir? Yes or no. Just yes or no. I have other questions.

Mr. NAATZ. Yes.

Mr. POWELL. Yes.

Mr. SCHUTT. I don't believe that——

Mr. SABLAN. Yes or no.

Mr. SCHUTT. I don't believe, with the factual premise of the question.

Mr. SABLAN. Please, I have other questions. I only have 5 minutes. Yes or no.

Mr. SCHUTT. It is not a taxpayer burden, no.

Mr. MATSON. Yes, it is a taxpayer burden.

Mr. SABLAN. All right. Mr. Naatz, in your written testimony, sir, you drew attention to the fact that half of all active wells are found on just five refuges. But it is also a fact that oil and gas development can be found on nearly half of the Nation's 562 refuges. Why don't you think that people who hunt, fish, and enjoy the outdoors at these refuges deserve to have a system in place for preventing and cleaning up oil spills?

Mr. NAATZ. Congressman, the issue is that they do have a system. The current system is nimble, it addresses what is going on.

Again, it is important to remember that that is a property right that largely happened as the Federal Government came over the top of what was happening. So these are private owners who have that property right.

Again, we want to stress that there is a system in place: the State regulatory agencies. And for every area, the States have that——

Mr. SABLAN. OK, there is a system in place. But it must not be working, because that is what GAO is suggesting in their report, that we look into this, and Fish and Wildlife Service should look into this, and make sure that there is a way to make these things work. That is why we are in a hearing today. Don't you think?

Mr. NAATZ. Having sat here, the GAO reports that we are talking about is a little bit like the Bible. You take the——

Mr. SABLAN. I like the Bible, sir. I like the Bible.

Mr. NAATZ. Because I would tell you it also says that Congress should be the one that finally makes the decision, that any of these decisions that you are talking about should have Congress really make those decisions, because you are talking about important rights. You are talking about property rights, which I think we all want to protect.

Mr. SABLAN. You are a smarter guy, so I won't debate with you, sir. You are going to probably win it. But I like the Bible. I am sorry.

Mr. Matson, if my oil—I really like to have oil, sir—but if my oil is underneath your land, I have a right to access it. But don't you also have a right to require me to enter into a legally binding contract to access your land and clean up any damage I cause?

Mr. MATSON. I sure hope I would have the right, as a private land owner. I certainly expect that right to be conferred to the Fish and Wildlife Service.

I want to assure the Chairman that I have no intention of misleading or perjuring myself here, in front of the Congress, and that all those pictures are from national wildlife refuges, where I said they were. But, even if they weren't from national wildlife refuges, they are real pictures. And, clearly, some system somewhere is broken. And given that most of that activity is regulated by the States, I would argue that State regulation currently is likely inadequate.

Finally, on the GAO debate, whether they called for Congress, they said the Fish and Wildlife Service needs to set reasonable conditions regarding these rights, and to report the results of their determination to Congress—and I have it right here—and then they finally said to go to Congress for any additional authority they might need, above and beyond that.

Mr. SABLAN. I thank you. I have no further questions, Mr. Chairman.

Dr. FLEMING. The gentleman yields back. Mr. Young?

Mr. YOUNG. Thank you, Mr. Chairman. Mr. Schutt, you have been involved with trying to develop your leases. What has the Fish and Wildlife done without these regulations to help you get this done?

Mr. SCHUTT. Thank you, Mr. Young, for your question. You know, the Fish and Wildlife Service, in the Kenai National Wildlife Refuge, has done a more than adequate job in protecting surface resources. I think they have the threat of a variety of regulatory and legal tools already at their disposal, and——

Mr. YOUNG. OK, let me clarify what I am saying, have they been helpful in getting your oil developed?

Mr. SCHUTT. Absolutely not.

Mr. YOUNG. OK. What have they required you to do, even without these regulations that are being proposed?

Mr. SCHUTT. Basically, any action by one of my lessees on the refuge, if it is allowed at all, is required to go through a full EIS process. Whether—including the last one that one of my lessees went through, which was to develop a 2½ mile gravel—single-lane gravel road to a prospect site for a drilling location, went through a full EIS, although the no-action alternative was explicitly prohibited, because they knew that they could not say no, directly. But that was a 30-month EIS process for a 2½ mile, single-land gravel road.

Mr. YOUNG. OK. What I am leading up to, the gentleman from the Fish and Wildlife and the gentleman from the Defenders say, "We are not prohibiting you from developing your"—but the key doesn't fit. Can you imagine, with these new regulations, how long it would take you to try to find your rightfully owned oil, because they are imposing these new regulations? I would say maybe 25 years. You would have gray hair by then.

Mr. SCHUTT. Correct. I think, to be clear, they do occasionally say no to things that we don't agree that they can say no to. One recent example is, as you know, one of the preliminary steps for oil and gas exploration is the shooting of modern seismic to gather the subsurface data to identify prospects to be drilled. The Fish and Wildlife Service has not provided adequate access to the surface of the refuge for that non-intrusive seismic gathering activity. So I have a buffer around the exterior boundaries of my subsurface for which we cannot gain appropriate data.

Mr. YOUNG. They are prohibiting you from finding what is there?

Mr. SCHUTT. They are prohibiting us, through our lessees, from gathering data adequate to identify targets around the periphery of our subsurface holdings, yes.

Mr. YOUNG. And what regulation are they using for that?

Mr. SCHUTT. I am not sure.

Mr. YOUNG. Would you find that out for me? Because, again, they are taking away your subsurface right. If you don't know where it is—then you have not been able to use all the tools available, frankly, to do less damage. I mean——

Mr. SCHUTT. I believe, Mr. Young, that they are characterizing the activity that is required as being commercial activity in the refuge, and——

Mr. YOUNG. But oil drilling is commercial, is it not?

Mr. SCHUTT. Yes, it is.

Mr. YOUNG. But the other—finding it with seismic is commercial.

Now, this is an example, Mr. Chairman, again, of an agency that has gone amuck. This refuge, when it was developed, said subsurface and surface development of oil would take place and could take place, and now they are changing the rules.

Mr. SCHUTT. Correct. The northern refuge was formed out of a compromise between CIRI, the State of Alaska, and the U.S. Government. It was a highly negotiated document, and the rules have changed, or are being attempted to change at this point. We gave up a tremendous amount of rights under the Alaska Native Claims Settlement Act to obtain the 200,000-plus acres we have of subsurface within the Northern Kenai National Wildlife Refuge. That allowed the conversion of the moose range into the refuge, as we have it today.

Mr. YOUNG. And that was the law we passed in Congress, a law that you thought was going to be implemented. And now we have an executive agency changing the law of Congress.

Mr. SCHUTT. Correct.

Mr. YOUNG. What is wrong with America today. We are now being run by a monarchy of agencies supported by outside interest groups that don't know one side from the backside. Very, very frustrating to America, as far as I am concerned.

And as long as I sit in this seat, we are going to get those oil fields developed that were guaranteed under the Act of Congress to Alaska Natives. That is the right that we should have. I am done with this.

Dr. FLEMING. The gentleman yields. Mr. McAllister is recognized.

Mr. MCALLISTER. Thank you, Mr. Chairman. I am going to be looking for that key, Mr. Young, to see if we can fit that hole before this is over with.

Mr. Matson, to go back to those pictures that you showed—and, it is one of these things, I see those pictures and I understand how—a picture is worth a thousand words. But yet you come here before this committee today and show these pictures. Do you know when those repairs were made, the garbage bags, for instance? Do you know when it was made, prior to when you took the picture?

Mr. MATSON. That garbage bag picture was taken just a couple of months ago. And I believe it is still unrepaired.

Mr. MCALLISTER. You believe it is still unrepaired.

Mr. MATSON. That was a Fish and Wildlife Service picture, not my own. And I was told that that repair has not been made yet.

Mr. MCALLISTER. OK. So you took a picture of someone who was innovative. And rather than leaving the fluid to drip on the ground, repaired it with duct tape and a garbage bag. And yet you seem to be very upset about that, not knowing if that repair was made that morning because they didn't have the right tools, and trust me, I come from Louisiana, where I know it is very inaccessible to get to some of these facilities where we drill for oil and all, and there is not a local pipe supply on every corner. So sometimes you have to make do what you can make do.

But yet we are damned if we do and we are damned if we don't. We take a garbage bag and fix it and keep it from leaking, and yet you are still not happy, and you come to Washington, DC, and testify before Congress, and want to throw fits because some guy took the initiative to keep from spilling fluids on the ground, and you want to use an example of how the system has run amuck.

Mr. MATSON. I have a similar picture from a year before that one with the same set-up. So they never came back to repair it.

Mr. MCALLISTER. Was it leaking? Did it get into the ground, or was it still working?

Mr. MATSON. [No response.]

Mr. MCALLISTER. Fair question.

Mr. MATSON. I don't have an answer.

Mr. MCALLISTER. It was contained, was it not?

Mr. MATSON. With a very strong garbage bag, I guess.

Mr. MCALLISTER. I don't care if it is a strong garbage bag, or if it was——

Mr. MATSON. Anybody can come there, a storm can come, can punch the garbage bag, and there is a spill. Done.

Mr. MCALLISTER. Could have. Should have. Would have. It didn't. What I am saying is——

Mr. MATSON. Do you want a garbage bag repair on a well on your property?

Mr. MCALLISTER. Absolutely, before it runs on the ground. But I would hope they would come back and the proper maintenance would be taken.

Mr. MATSON. Exactly.

Mr. MCALLISTER. But I can take a picture at any time of anybody—I can take a picture of a vehicle with wire and bubble gum, but it is still working. That doesn't mean I want to drive it to California. But as long as it gets me home at the end of the night, I am good.

I am just saying you come up here with these pictures, and you try to blast that this industry is not taking care. Look, there are bad apples in every bunch of apples you pick. You went to the grocery store, and they are sitting on the shelf, and they just haven't been sold yet. I get that. I understand that we need to continue to do and improve, and you are sitting on the panel with three guys that are trying to make sure that the regulations are being imposed, and they are doing the right thing. You can't always fix—we can't legislate zero risk out of everything, and that is the truth of it.

But I understand your wanting to protect wildlife. And, look, I love the great outdoors, and I live in Louisiana, Sportsman's Paradise, and I love it, too. But I am not for giving ducks and deer weapons to shoot back at me. I am about protecting their habitats that they have, and we have done that. We have plentiful wildlife there.

But it just aggravates me that the body of Congress would be wasted with someone coming up and taking pictures of something that shows that it is fixed—it may not be fixed the way you want it, it may not be used by these high-dollar couplings and aluminum brass thread, whatever you want to put on them, but it is fixed, and it is not leaking, and you represent a picture here and you show, "Look at what has happened." You don't know if it was fixed that morning, before you got there. You don't know if they been using this for—you know what? We found the best line of garbage

64

bags there are, and they are better than any of the pipes you can go buy down at the pipe supply store.

But the fact of the matter is it is not leaking on the ground. And that is what you want to turn your testimony into, some pictures portraying the innovation of what America is. And I challenge you to—and I did see some sheen going off on the water, and you are absolutely right, that needs to be cleaned up, it needs to be mitigated, it needs to be taken care of. That is in everything, that is in every industry. But out of the thousands of wells across this Nation, you brought us four pictures.

Mr. MATSON. I could have taken up my entire 5 minutes with pictures. I totally get what you are saying, I respect what you are saying. I guess—and there are regulations specifically affecting those bad apples. Responsible operators have nothing to fear with these regulations that they are proposing.

Mr. MCALLISTER. OK. Then my questions to you other three are, do you ever try to weed out the bad apples and make sure you only have good apples in the industry?

Mr. NAATZ. Again, Congressman, we always are working to have the best standards, and our operators operate that way. Are we 100 percent perfect? No. But those are regulated, and we address that. So, certainly, we always understand that there are going to be operators that need—issues need to be addressed, and we try to do that.

Mr. POWELL. I think every day in Louisiana I see examples of operators solving these issues. It is almost impossible to regulate risk out of it without regulating the industry away. But I do see the operators solving these issues on a daily basis and complying with the regulations that are already there.

Mr. SCHUTT. We are extremely careful in the lessees that we allow to operate on our leases. I believe that, at the end of the day, with the environmental rules as they are written, if there is an environmental problem, we, as the lessor and beneficial royalty owner, could share in the pain of reclamation and remediation activity. So we are careful to make sure that our operators are responsible, good apples, and that they are well capitalized to take care of any problems they may cause on our leases.

Mr. MCALLISTER. I appreciate that. And I know I am running over, Chairman, but one more second.

I just want to tell you, I appreciate the innovativeness and trying to do what is right. And I come from a business background. I don't come from sitting at a desk, trying to write laws and legislate the risk out of everything. I come from getting stuff done and doing it.

And I guess, Mr. Matson, I am not trying to attack you or be on top of you, but it just aggravates the fire out of me to see pictures brought up here of someone trying to correct the problem. And it may not be the way that you want it done. But at the end of the day, you showed me pictures of a duct-taped fitting that was not leaking. You showed me pictures of a garbage bag capturing the fluids that you didn't want leaked. And yet, that seems to be your basis to stand on. And I guess it is a little frustrating for me, because I come from the business world of getting things done, and trying to create jobs, and make things happen for Americans. And

I didn't have the luxury to be hired by wildlife. I am not an attorney for the ducks.

But I do believe that they have their place to be, and that we should protect them at all costs. And I always believe in being a true conservationist. But don't attack an industry on what I view as being innovative, and not being detrimental. And, absolutely, I think those problems should be addressed, and they should be fixed with the proper methods. But let's give credit where credit is due. At least somebody took the initiative to make sure that it wasn't worse than what it could have been. And I yield back my time.

Dr. FLEMING. The gentleman yields back. I will open up the dais for one more question, and I will recognize myself first.

I have two comments. One, back to the pictures. Again, that is an old, old technique used to create emotion, again, without the full context, without a full evaluation and examination that is done by both parties and presented to us. This would be considered, in a court of law, prejudicial to show pictures such as that.

The other thing that is important, there was a little bit of discussion about, well, what did the GAO say. Did the GAO say that this is up to Fisheries and Wildlife, or to Congress? Well, I will just give you a quote: "We believe it is for Congress, not"—this is GAO, in their report, 2007—"We believe it is for Congress, not DOI, to weigh the needs of the refuge lands and interests of mineral owners and, ultimately, to determine what oversight authority would be appropriate." I think that is pretty clear language. And you can lift that out of any book, any size, and that says it all. GAO says, "It is up for you, Congress."

And we are here, representing the people. That is our job. When you have a government, as Mr. Young says, that wants to function in a dictatorial way to determine, through its own power and its own will, what is right for Americans, then we are no longer a country of democracy. We are no longer a representative democracy, a republic, if you will. We are a government that is really run by one branch, rather than three branches, as our founding fathers determined.

So, I would be happy to—again, Mr. Naatz, if you would like to comment on that, that goes back to some of the things that you were saying.

Mr. NAATZ. Mr. Chairman, we couldn't agree with you more. And, if you look at the report—and again, as you look at the mineral rights that are owned, they are private mineral rights. And in those issues, again, we believe very strongly if you look at the GAO report, just what you read, those are issues that Congress would have to deal with——

Dr. FLEMING. Well, the right to own property, doesn't that go to the very essence of the Constitution of the United States, private property rights?

Mr. NAATZ. Yes, sir.

Dr. FLEMING. I mean that is what sets us apart, particularly back in 1776, when we declared our independence and later wrote the Constitution. That, above all things, set America apart from every other Nation in history, that we recognize the private property rights of individuals. And even today, the right to own a home, to own mineral rights—again, subsurface—all of these things are so important. And sometimes Government does have to step in, but only as a last resort, not because some agency or some bureau feels like—some service feels like—"Hey, we don't have enough to do, we are going to go take for ourselves more power, regulate in areas we have never regulated before, and we will demand from Congress to pay for it," which is really the taxpayers, the hardworking taxpayers, to pay for that.

And then to, in a supercilious way, do this when, in fact, these regulations, these regulatory mechanisms, are already in place. So we are only—it is as though the Federal Government has run out of things to do. Now we've got to go back and do what the States have been doing. That is ludicrous.

But, anyway, I appreciate your comments on that. And I will be happy to yield to the Ranking Member. He is the only other Member left on the dais for any comments or questions you may have for us today.

Mr. SABLAN. Thank you, Mr. Chairman. Actually, I am going to associate myself with Chairman Fleming's just recent statement that—which is why I said in my opening statement that I thanked him for holding today's hearing. Because any time we uncover a situation where private interests get the fist and Federal taxpayers get stuck with the bill, then this subcommittee needs to pay attention and maybe take action. And that is why I am very grateful that we are having today's hearing. And I yield back, Mr. Chairman, and I thank everyone for taking part in today.

Dr. FLEMING. I thank the gentleman, and thank him for his comments.

Before closing, I would like to ask unanimous consent to submit for the hearing record the letter I wrote to Director Dan Ashe on April 23, 2014, and a statement for the record by the Arctic Slope Regional Corporation.

[No response.]

Dr. FLEMING. Hearing no objection, so ordered.

[The information submitted for the record by Dr. Fleming follows:]

LETTER SUBMITTED FOR THE RECORD BY DR. FLEMING

CONGRESS OF THE UNITED STATES,
WASHINGTON, DC,
APRIL 23, 2014.

Hon. DANIEL M. ASHE, *Director*,
U.S. Fish and Wildlife Service,
1848 C Street, N.W.,
Washington, DC 20240.

DEAR DIRECTOR ASHE:

On February 24, 2014, the U.S. Fish and Wildlife Service ("the Service") announced the opening of a 60-day comment period to seek input on managing non-Federal oil and gas development on National Wildlife Refuge System (NWRS) lands. The Service provided the justification that it is responding to Government Accountability Office (GAO) reports from 2003 and 2007, which criticize the Service for failing to adequately catalog and manage existing wells.

Before the Service puts forth any new regulations, I request that the Service work with Congress to identify the extent of its authority under existing statutes, per the recommendation of GAO. In addition, the Service should be cognizant of the following principles:

- Primacy of State regulation and enforcement: States have unique insights into the lands and people within their borders, and the Service should defer to existing State regulations and State enforcement authorities.
- Avoidance of duplication: The Service should not duplicate functions already conducted by States. In cases where a State regulator is physically unable to inspect the wells within the refuges, the Service may consider ways to supplement the State's effort, but the Service should not create a new regime that duplicates the State's resources and efforts.
- Preservation of access: The Service has made clear its commitment to honoring the private property rights of subsurface rights holders. However, the Service should not consider any new barriers to access through delaying the approval process or expanding requirements in a burdensome manner. The Service should presume issuance of the necessary permits to honor property rights.

I would discourage the Service from assuming that it must mirror other Federal agencies such as the National Park Service or the Forest Service. All too often, these agencies have overstepped their bounds and impinged on the purview of State regulators. Rather, I urge the Service to defer the issuance of any new regulation until it has followed GAO's recommendations to work with Congress on determining the extent of its authority.

Sincerely,

JOHN FLEMING, M.D.,
Chairman,
Subcommittee on Fisheries, Wildlife,
Oceans and Insular Affairs.

———

ARCTIC SLOPE REGIONAL CORPORATION,
ANCHORAGE, ALASKA,
MAY 20, 2014.

Hon. JOHN FLEMING, *Chairman,*
House Subcommittee on Fisheries, Wildlife, Oceans and Insular Affairs,
1324 Longworth House Office Building,
Washington, DC 20515.

DEAR CHAIRMAN FLEMING:

On behalf of Arctic Slope Regional Corporation (ASRC), I write to offer our views on oil and gas activities within our Nation's wildlife refuge system, the subject of the subcommittee's hearing on May 20, 2014.

My comments focus on our continuing frustration, shared by the State of Alaska, Alaska's congressional delegation, and the majority of the residents of our region, with the long-delayed efforts in Congress to allow responsible development of the significant oil and gas resources within the northernmost of U.S. wildlife refuges, the Arctic National Wildlife Refuge (ANWR).

Who We Are

ASRC is an Alaska Native-owned corporation established under the Alaska Native Claims Settlement Act of 1971 (''ANCSA''). Under ANCSA, Iñupiat Eskimos living on the North Slope of Alaska in 1971 were enrolled as shareholders in ASRC. ASRC has since issued additional shares to our descendants, and currently has a shareholder base of approximately 11,000 people. ASRC represents the varied interests of its Iñupiat shareholders, including many of the residents of Alaska's North Slope. We are committed to protecting the environment, the land, and the culture of the Iñupiat people.

ANWR: A Refuge Set Aside to Ensure a Balance Between Conservation and Oil and Gas

What we now know as ANWR was originally established in 1960, when President Eisenhower's Secretary of the Interior, Fred Seaton, signed a Public Land Order establishing the 8.9 million acre Arctic National Wildlife Range. After years of debate over the fate of the Range, in 1980, Congress enacted the Alaska National Interest Lands Conservation Act (''ANILCA''). ANILCA doubled the size of the Range, renamed it the Arctic National Wildlife Refuge, and designated eight million acres (most of the original Range) as wilderness.

The northernmost 1.5 million acres of ANWR, the Coastal Plain, was designated in Section 1002 of ANILCA, and is now referred to as the 1002 Area. Although ANILCA set aside much of ANWR in protected status, Section 1002 reserved judgment on the future of the Coastal Plain, setting the area aside for further assessment of its oil and gas development potential and its fish and wildlife resources.

In 1987, after 6 years of environmental, geologic, and economic study required by ANILCA, the Department of the Interior recommended that the 1002 Area be opened to responsible oil and gas development. Since completion of that report, numerous wells have been drilled and oil fields discovered near ANWR. The U.S. Geological Service estimates that a median of 10.6 billion barrels of oil lie within the Coastal Plain. By way of comparison, when the Prudhoe Bay oil field was discovered in 1968, it was estimated to contain about 9.6 billion barrels of recoverable oil. In 2012, oil produced from the field surpassed the 12 billion barrel mark. The Prudhoe Bay oil field will fuel Alaska's economy for at least 50 years. The 1002 Area could fuel our economy for another 50 years, or more. However, in Section 1003 of ANILCA, Congress prohibited any development of oil and gas in the 1002 Area until such development is authorized by an act of Congress.

In the 113th Congress, legislation introduced by the Congressman Don Young would permit leasing within 1002 Area of ANWR. H.R. 49 would limit the total surface acreage covered by production and support facilities to less than 2,000 acres on the Coastal Plain. Several facilities would be connected by pipelines. But the footprint of development in ANWR would be a fraction of that in neighboring Prudhoe Bay. Today, horizontal drilling means fewer wells, with producers able to reach much farther from small drilling pads. Better land use planning allows for consolidation of common facilities. Gravel roads and drill pads often can be replaced by winter ice roads and drill pads, which melt without leaving a trace of human activity.

A Matter of Fairness

ANWR is roughly the size of South Carolina or Maine. It is a beautiful place, worthy of appropriate protections, but it is not an empty or unpopulated place. More than 200 Iñupiat people live in the Village of Kaktovik, on the boundary of the Area. All of ANWR is part of our traditional homeland and much of the land around the Village remains in Native ownership today.

ASRC and Kaktovik Iñupiat Corporation ("KIC"), the Native Corporation for the Village of Kaktovik, own more than 92,000 subsurface and surface acres, respectively, within ANWR's Coastal Plain. These lands hold significant potential for onshore oil and gas development. However, as a result of Section 1003 of ANILCA, development of these important economic resources remains off limits until further act of Congress.

As early as November 2009, at the White House Tribal Nations Conference, President Obama acknowledged that, "Promises were broken. You were told your lands, your religion, your cultures, your languages were not yours to keep." The U.S. Fish and Wildlife Service (USFWS) now appears to be taking steps (without clear legal authority, we might add) to recommend that the Coastal Plain should be designated Wilderness. [1] If, in fact, the USFWS intends to make this recommendation, this Administration's actions will fly in the face of promises that were made to the only Native Americans that live within the Federal boundaries of the 19.6 million acres of ANWR. If the Coastal Plain were to be designated Wilderness, Kaktovik would be surrounded, making the villagers essentially refugees on their own land. The residents of the Village of Kaktovik already are deprived of substantial economic op-

---

[1] The USFWS is updating its comprehensive conservation plan ("CCP") for ANWR. ASRC and the North Slope Borough submitted joint comments to the USFWS, in which we urged that the USFWS not take any action through the CCP revision process that would, directly or indirectly, impact or foreclose the economic opportunities associated with the potential for future development of the enormous oil and gas reserves in the Coastal Plain or that would place additional regulatory or permitting restrictions on local residents that depend on the Refuge for their subsistence needs.

The draft CCP and draft Environmental Impact Statement (DEIS) described and evaluated six alternatives for the long-term management of the Refuge. These alternatives range from a "no action" alternative providing for the continuation of current management practices to a far-reaching alternative that would recommend virtually the entire Refuge, including the nearly 1.5 million acre Coastal Plain, for designation under the Wilderness Act and four additional rivers for designation as Wild and Scenic Rivers. The draft CCP and DEIS did not identify a preferred alternative.

A revised CCP and final EIS were scheduled to be released 2 years ago. Absent any explanation for the delay in releasing these documents, we can only presume that the Administration is sitting on a final CCP that recommends setting aside the 1002 Area as Wilderness.

portunity because without further act of Congress, the Coastal Plain of ANWR is closed to oil and gas development.

Congress has the authority to authorize measured oil and gas leasing within ANWR—subject to targeted environmental regulations—which will provide economic benefits within the region, the State, and the country. We know that drilling in ANWR is a controversial issue, and how we go about doing it properly is a matter of public debate. Our congressional delegation is at the table, as are we.

Congress must act if the Iñupiat people, who once held aboriginal title to all of the North Slope's 56 million acres, are to be permitted to develop their own lands within the Coastal Plain of ANWR.

Reasonable People Can Find Common Ground on ANWR

In 2009, Senators Lisa Murkowski and Mark Begich introduced the "ANWR No Surface Occupancy Western Arctic Coastal Plain Domestic Energy Security Act", which would have authorized directional drilling into ANWR, thereby allowing for development of part of ANWR's oil and gas reserves without *any footprint whatsoever* in the Coastal Plain. The bill failed to advance.

The Iñupiat people have the greatest stake in preserving our heritage, and for this reason, we have debated oil and gas development, as any open and thoughtful community would. We are a practical people, and we seek to understand other points of view and we look for compromise. We cannot understand why some special interest groups would oppose even directional drilling under the Coastal Plain where such drilling would result in no surface activity within the Refuge.

By once again submitting our testimony to this committee, we appeal to all of you, who were elected to come here to represent the best interests of your communities and of the entire country, to come to the table with our elected representatives and our communities to pursue Federal legislation that authorizes a reasonable approach to oil and gas development in the northernmost of U.S. wildlife refuges.

A founding principle of ASRC is respect for the Iñupiat heritage. We adhere to the traditional values of protecting the land, the environment and the culture of the Iñupiat. That is why we worked with Congressman Young and our Senators to include a wide range of special environmental protective measures in legislation introduced over the years that would open the Coastal Plain to oil and gas leasing. Congressman Young's most recent bill, H.R. 49, retains those protections, and we thank him for his continuing commitment to responsible development in the Coastal Plain of ANWR.

The potential benefit of opening the Coastal Plain to leasing is enormous. 10.6 billion barrels of oil would support our local economy—and the State of Alaska's economy—for many decades, providing funding for education, infrastructure, and health and social services. The potential cost of not opening Coastal Plain is enormous, too. Responsible new development is desperately needed ensure future flows through the Trans-Alaska Pipeline System, which is operating at just one-third of its original capacity.

ANWR is a place that can support both measured development and landscape-scale conservation. But ANWR is not a monolithic thing—it is a collection of diverse places that are united by a line drawn on a map. One of those places—the 1002 Area—offers great potential for the people who live in Kaktovik and throughout the North Slope Borough, for the State of Alaska, and for the United States. Thank you for your support.

Sincerely,

REX A. ROCK, SR.,
President and CEO.

———

Dr. FLEMING. While I did not mention the National Park Service in my comments, let me be clear. There is a fundamental difference between refuge lands and those managed by the National Park Service. Any effort to recreate or transform a refuge into a national park is inappropriate and wrong.

I want to thank Members and staff for their contributions to this hearing. And again I want to thank our panel, both first and second panel, for coming in today and giving their testimony and answering the hard questions.

There being no further business, without objection, the subcommittee stands adjourned.

[Whereupon, at 4:10 p.m., the subcommittee was adjourned.]

[ADDITIONAL MATERIALS SUBMITTED FOR THE RECORD]

QUESTIONS SUBMITTED FOR THE RECORD TO U.S. FISH AND WILDLIFE SERVICE

Question 1. What is your current regulatory authority over oil and gas operations within the refuge system? Please cite specific language in P.L. 105–57.

Answer. Section 5(b)(5)—"Issue regulations to carry out this Act"

Section 5(a)(4)(A) & (B)—"In administering the System, the Secretary shall——

(A) provide for the conservation of fish, wildlife, and plants, and their habitats within the System;

(B) ensure that the biological integrity, diversity, and environmental health of the System are maintained for the benefit of present and future generations of Americans;"

Question 2. Of the 1,700 active wells within the national wildlife refuge system, how many are oil wells?

Answer. Based on our best available information the U.S. Fish and Wildlife Service (Service) estimates there are approximately 257 active wells that produce primarily oil and approximately 8 active wells that produce a combination of both oil and gas.

Question 3. Do you have a database on the nature and extent of oil and gas activities within the national wildlife refuge system?

Answer. Yes. The Service has a database that was developed from information maintained by the Environmental Protection Agency (EPA) that was collected from each State. The Service extracted data on refuges from the EPA dataset in 2011 to compile our database.

Question 4. Of the 1,700 active wells, how many are reserved mineral rights vs. outstanding mineral rights?

Answer. The Service does not have access to this information.

Question 5. Other than those oil and gas operations that existed prior to acquisi-tion, how many new oil and gas activities have begun operations within the refuge system within the last 20 years? Please provide a list.

Answer. Since 1994 at least 667 wells were drilled within the Refuge System:

FWS Region / State / NWR	GAS	OIL	OIL & GAS	OTHER	Grand Total
Region 2	87	20	2	2	111
NM	2				2
BITTER LAKE NWR	2				2
OK	1				1
OPTIMA NWR	1				1
TX	84	20	2	2	108
ANAHUAC NWR	2	1			3
ARANSAS NWR	11				11
ATTWATER PRAIRIE CHICKEN	12				12
BRAZORIA NWR	3				3
CADDO LAKE NWR	2	1		1	4
HAGERMAN NWR	2	15		1	18
LAGUNA ATASCOSA NWR	1				1
LOWER RIO GRANDE VALLEY NWR	44		2		46
MCFADDIN NWR	1	2			3
SAN BERNARD NWR	4	1			5
TRINITY RIVER NWR	2				2
Region 3		1		1	2
IN		1		1	2
PATOKA RIVER NWR		1		1	2
Region 4	122	73	3	332	530
LA	122	73	3	332	530
ATCHAFALAYA NWR	1	5		7	13
BAYOU COCODRIE NWR				8	8
BAYOU SAUVAGE NWR				1	1
BAYOU TECHE NWR	1			5	6
BLACK BAYOU LAKE NWR	3			6	9
BRETON NWR				1	1
CAMERON PRAIRIE NWR				4	4
CAT ISLAND NWR	1				1
CATAHOULA NWR	1	2		10	13
D'ARBONNE NWR	11			83	94
DELTA NWR	28	26	1	25	80
GRAND COTE NWR				1	1
LACASSINE NWR	8	3	1	11	23

LAKE OPHELIA NWR				10	10
MANDALAY NWR	2	1		9	12
RED RIVER NWR	2	12		13	27
SABINE NWR	13	20	1	21	55
ST. CATHERINE CREEK NWR				1	1
TENSAS RIVER NWR		2		13	15
UPPER OUACHITA NWR	51	2		103	156
Region 5		1			1
WV		1			1
OHIO RIVER ISLANDS NWR		1			1
Region 6	22		1		23
MT	22				22
BOWDOIN NWR	1				1
BOWDOIN NWR	12				12
HEWITT LAKE NWR	9				9
ND			1		1
LAKE ILO NWR			1		1
Grand Total	231	95	6	335	667

Question 6. In 2007, the Government Accountability Office recommended that the Service hire 32 refuge oil and gas specialists, 7 Regional Coordinators and a 6-member Mineral Regional Team. How many of those positions are currently filled?

Answer. The Service has hired a total of 13 oil and gas-related positions including: 4 national level staff which includes a program coordinator, a National Environmental Policy Act (NEPA) specialist, environmental contaminants specialist, and a petroleum engineer; 4 oil and gas specialists in the Service's Southwest Region; 1 oil and gas specialist, 1 law enforcement officer, and 1 regional energy coordinator in the Service's Southeast Region; 1 regional energy coordinator in the Service's Mountain-Prairie Region; and 1 oil and gas specialist in the Service's Alaska Region.

Question 7. GAO also recommended in 2003 that the Service establish an inventory of oil and gas wells and infrastructure on refuge lands. What is the status of that comprehensive inventory?

Answer. The Service has assembled a database of over 5,000 oil and gas wells that occur on refuge system fee title lands. To keep this dataset current, the Service will continually update the dataset with data collected from States.

Question 8. Does the Service have a national tracking system for oil and gas activities within the refuge system?

Answer. The Service has regional oil and gas coordinators/representatives that collate and share oil and gas data within the Service. This national team continues to develop new tools such as a national spills database, oil and gas well and pipeline database; inspection and monitoring database, and other electronic inspection and monitoring forms, guidance and other support tools.

Question 9. Does the Service charge rent or access fees to energy companies who desire to utilize their reserved or outstanding mineral rights? What restrictions does the Service place on those companies?

Answer. Typically, we do not charge rent or access fees to companies to utilize their mineral rights. However, if a company needs a right-of-way, the Service charges fees for that right-of-way. A mineral owner has a legal right to access their minerals; but if the owner needs to cross lands that the owner does not own, a right-of-way may be required. For example, if a new access route is developed such as a road.

In regard to restrictions, the Service could apply conditions as part of the Special Use Permit process or terms and conditions as part of the right-of-way process. The most commonly applied condition is a timing restriction. This restricts certain activities for a specific period of time, such as during nesting season for migratory birds. Other conditions are used to reduce environmental impacts, to ensure compliance with various Federal laws and regulations. For example, the Service may restrict the location of the placement of a well if a cultural survey indicates that there is a site eligible for the register of Historic Places.

Question 10. Can the Fish and Wildlife Service deny access to these subsurface minerals that it does not own? If you were to deny access, wouldn't that be a "takings" and a violation of the company's 5th Amendment constitutional rights?

Answer. The Service ordinarily will not deny access to subsurface minerals that it does not own. A total denial of access would likely constitute a compensable taking under the Fifth Amendment. See *Lingle* v. *Chevron U.S.A. Inc.*, 544 U.S. 528, 539–40 (2005); *Lucas* v. *S.C. Coastal Council*, 505 U.S. 1003, 1018–19 (1992). Whether restricted access to subsurface minerals amounts to a compensable taking would depend on the specific facts involved. See *Tahoe-Sierra Preservation Council, Inc.* v. *Tahoe Regional Planning Agency*, 535 U.S. 302, 325–28 (2002); *Penn Central Transp. Co.* v. *New York City*, 438 U.S. 104, 124 (1978). If denial of access is found to constitute a taking, the Fifth Amendment would not forbid the taking, but the owner would be entitled to just compensation.

Question 11. Does the Service have oil and gas production figures for operations within the refuge system? How did you determine that energy companies owed the Service $2.8 million in royalty payments in FY13?

Answer. The Refuge System does not track production figures on non-Federal minerals. These figures are proprietary information. The $2.8 million in royalty payments received in Fiscal Year 2013 was from Federal mineral leases, not from oil production related to privately held subsurface mineral rights. Federal mineral leases are managed by the Bureau of Land Management (BLM) and the revenue is collected by the Department of the Interior's Office of Natural Resources Revenue (ONRR).

Question 12. Have there been any major oil spills (over 1,000 barrels of oil) from an exploration or production well within the refuge system? What does the Service define as a major oil spill in terms of barrels lost?

Answer. The Service is not aware of a spill over 1,000 barrels of oil (bbl) due to an exploration or production well within the Refuge System in the past 5 years. There have been numerous smaller spills on Refuge System lands that cumulatively surpass 1,000 bbl.

The Service does not have a specific definition of a "major spill." Any spill that is not contained could result in significant resource damage, depending on the habitat impacted and the species present.

Question 13. During the past 10 years, how many total barrels of oil have been spilled from oil wells within the refuge system? Please specify if the spills came from active wells or abandoned wells. Also, who paid for the cost of cleaning up these spills?

Answer. Most spills do not occur at the wellhead—the majority of spills are production-related, from flowlines, headers, facilities, or storage vessels.

Most oil and gas activity within the Refuge System occurs within the Service's Southeast Region, and the Service focuses its efforts in this region. Therefore our best information to answer this question is from this region. Approximately 800 bbl have been spilled on refuges in the Southeast Region over the last 10 years, based on file records and refuge staff interviews, for actively producing wells, At this point in time we lack comprehensive information on spills in refuges across the Nation and spills from abandoned wells.

Where wells are actively producing oil or gas, the responsible party pays for the cost of clean-up. However, the largest reported spill from a single well, a plugged and abandoned well, on Refuge System lands happened at St. Catherine Creek National Wildlife Refuge. For this spill, there was no responsible party identified, so EPA directed the cleanup using funds from the Oil Spill Liability Trust Fund.

Question 14. How many barrels have been spilled because of pipelines within the refuge system? Who paid for the cost of cleaning up these spills?

Answer. Many spills go unreported because the spill reporting requirements vary from State to State. The Service can provide specific examples of spills, but we are unable to provide a comprehensive list due to the varying nature of State reporting requirements. A revised national level regulation would standardize this reporting requirement.

Here are two recent examples:

In the Service's Southwest Region, a pipeline ruptured on Deep Fork National Wildlife Refuge on April 7, 2011. This was discovered by another pipeline company employee and was reported to the Refuge. According to the EPA's National Response Center report, an estimated 50 bbl was released. The leak had been ongoing for several months, so actual total amount of oil released was unable to be determined. EPA was notified and responded to the cleanup in coordination with Service. The Service was reimbursed for our expenses through the Oil Spill Liability Trust Fund.

On Delta National Wildlife Refuge in Service's Southeast Region, Chevron had a 400 bbl spill on the Refuge. Chevron paid for all cleanup and restoration efforts.

Question 15. The Service has indicated that abandoned oil and gas infrastructure represents a major environmental hazard within the refuge system. What is your current authority in dealing with abandoned rigs or equipment?

Answer. Two existing, but limited, regulatory provisions are applicable to such abandoned property:

50 CFR § 29.32 provides that "structures and equipment must be removed from the area when the need for them has ended."

50 CFR § 28.41 provides that "any property abandoned or left unattended without authority on any national wildlife refuge for a period in excess of 72 hours is subject to removal. The expense of the removal shall be borne by the person owning or claiming ownership of the property. Such property is subject to sale or other disposal after 3 months, in accordance with section 203m of the Federal Property and Administrative Services Act of 1959, as amended (40 U.S.C. 484m), and regulations issued thereunder. Former owners may apply within 3 years for reimbursement for such property, subject to disposal and storage costs and similar expenses, upon sufficient proof of ownership."

However, there are no penalties applicable for failing to comply with these regulatory requirements, nor does either provision provide a requirement to post bonds to cover the costs of removal and property restoration. Thus, if the mineral interest owner fails to remove the property, the Service must seek injunctive relief in court or to remove the property itself at taxpayer expense.

Question 16. Who pays for the clean-up of oil spills from abandoned wells? Have you obtained any money from the Oil Pollution Liability Trust Fund?

Answer. The cost of cleanup of oil spills from abandoned wells, where no identifiable, viable party can be identified, can be paid by the State or the Service. In addition, the Oil Spill Liability Trust Fund, which is administered by the United States Coast Guard, is a potential source of funding for clean-up of oil spills when there is a discharge, or substantial threat of discharge, to waters of the United States or adjoining shorelines. The Service has received monies for cleanup from this fund.

Question 17. Do you aggressively seek reimbursement from the owners of the abandoned, plugged or shut-in wells when they cause environmental damage?

Answer. When the Service is made aware of a problematic abandoned well we actively seek reimbursement from the owners of the abandoned wells where those owners have violated Federal statutes. However, often there is no solvent owner to pursue for damages. In those cases, the cost of addressing the problems caused by the well is paid by taxpayers.

Question 18. On April 6, 2010, there was a 400 barrel oil spill from a pipeline at the Delta National Wildlife Refuge. What was the reaction and efforts by the pipeline owner to clean-up this spill?

Answer. The reaction to the spill at Delta National Wildlife Refuge by Chevron was immediate. An oil spill response organization was on site and cooperated from the initial notification of the spill to "close out," when the Delta National Wildlife Refuge staff was satisfied with the clean-up efforts.

Question 19. The initial public comment period on your Advanced Notice of Proposed Rulemaking closed on April 25, 2014. How many comments did you receive during that 60-day period? How many of those comments reflected the opinion that the Service *should not* proceed with new Federal regulations?

Answer. We received 47,454 comments on the Advanced Notice of Proposed Rulemaking (ANPR) during the comment period. The Service received 10 comments stating that the Service should not proceed with new regulations.

Question 20. How long will it take to review those comments and do you intend to complete an Environmental Impact Statement?

Answer. The Service reopened the comment period for an additional 30 days beginning June 9, 2014 and closing on July 9, 2014. We anticipate finalizing a report on those comments by the end of the summer of 2014. Along with the publication of the ANPR the Service announced a notice of intent to prepare an Environmental Impact Statement (EIS). It is too early to project when we will complete an EIS.

Question 21. Can you assure this committee that the Service will not apply for a Categorical Exclusion for these proposed regulations?

Answer. Yes. If the Service deems the responses to the ANPR/NOI justify a rulemaking, then the Service intends to proceed with a programmatic EIS, which would incorporate public feedback on the draft rule and subsequent NEPA analysis.

Question 22. When will the final rule be published and what is your target date for these regulations to be effective? Will you stipulate that any new regulations will be prospective in their authority?

Answer. We are in the very early stages of considering a rulemaking. It is too early to estimate the publication date of a potential final rule. Also, at this early stage, we cannot stipulate on whether any potential regulations would be prospective although we would give full consideration to that approach if we begin to develop proposed regulations.

Question 23. Did the Service receive directions, instructions or suggestions from the Department of the Interior, the Public Employees for Environmental Responsibility (PEER) or other nongovernmental organizations that it was time to more vigorously regulate these activities under refuge lands?

Answer. The Service received an inquiry from PEER in 2011 suggesting the Service update its oil and gas regulations. We have not received a request from the Department of the Interior or any nongovernmental organization outside of PEER prior to the opening of the comment period on the ANPR.

Question 24. Since the Service cannot deny access to these oil companies who own the minerals, aren't there limits on how much you can charge them in terms of an annual permit or what you call "reasonable" access fees?

Answer. The Service would not charge more than reasonable and customary permit or access fees as determined by those charged to operators by other oil and gas regulatory agencies and landowners.

Question 25. Do you intend to require annual inspections of both active and inactive wells? What is the cost of such an inspection?

Answer. We cannot state definitively whether any potential regulations would require annual inspections or what they would specifically entail. Monitoring of activity is integral to any regulatory program, and the frequency is dependent on the type of operations, environmental conditions, and other factors. It is reasonable to assume that monitoring could be expected on at least an annual basis. It is also reasonable to assume that inspections would be conducted by Service personnel, and therefore that operators would bear no out-of-pocket expense for the inspections themselves.

Question 26. Let's talk about the scope of these new regulations. Here is my hypothetical question: My family has been in the energy business for nearly 100 years. We have a number of oil wells that are drilled on our private property and because of horizontal drilling we are able to extract oil resources from subsurface lands we own under a national wildlife refuge. How will any new Federal regulations affect my oil and gas activities?

Answer. The Service is not contemplating regulation of activities beyond Refuge System boundaries, including the surface operations of wells that are directionally drilled from points outside a unit or the Refuge System boundary to points underneath it.

Question 27. Since the Service has a legitimate concern about abandoned wells and orphaned infrastructure equipment, why not confine your new regulations to these pressing problems?

Answer. By definition, orphaned wells have no responsible party, so there is no entity to regulate. Orphaned wells would be addressed outside of the currently contemplated regulation.

A comprehensive suite of revised regulations could prevent current operations from falling into disrepair and ultimately into an abandoned or orphan status.

Question 28. How many qualified oil and gas inspectors work for the Fish and Wildlife Service?

Answer. When the Service addresses the term "inspector", it is within the context of our current authorities. Our inspectors are biologists, refuge managers, refuge staff, and law enforcement officers. The Service has many staff on refuges that deal with a variety of damage issues not related to oil and gas as the destruction of refuge property, illegal dumping, etc. These staff also examine oil and gas infrastructure under our current regulatory authorities. They are looking for leaks, spills, physical problems, and poorly maintained equipment, among other issues. If we see problems outside our authority, we report those to the proper regulatory authority, such as the State permitting office.

Question 29. In the testimony of Mr. Steve Guertin, he indicated that the Service acquires refuge property, "with the least amount of property right necessary to carry out our primary mission." However, by trying to regulate adjacent private landowners attempting to access private mineral rights under a refuge, without ever touching the actual surface property owned by the Service, it appears that you are trying to apply an amount of authority that would be more reflective of having acquired the maximum amount of property rights. If the Service wants to regulate at this level, shouldn't the agency have acquired the entire property rights in the first place?

Answer. The Service is not contemplating regulation of activities outside the boundaries of Refuge System units. We are not contemplating regulations that would apply to adjacent private landowners attempting to access private mineral rights under a refuge without accessing refuge lands administered by the Service,

----

LETTER SUBMITTED FOR THE RECORD FROM THE STATE OF ALASKA, ANILCA IMPLEMENTATION PROGRAM TO THE U.S. FISH AND WILDLIFE SERVICE

STATE OF ALASKA,
ANCHORAGE, ALASKA,
APRIL 24, 2014.

U.S. Fish and Wildlife Service,
4401 N. Fairfax Drive,
Arlington, VA 22203.

TO WHOM IT MAY CONCERN:

The State of Alaska reviewed the February 24, 2014 Advanced Notice of Proposed Rulemaking and Notice of Intent to prepare a programmatic environmental impact statement (PEIS) regarding management of activities associated with non-Federal oil and gas development occurring on lands and waters of the National Wildlife Refuge System. The following comments represent the consolidated views of the State's resource agencies.

The notice indicates the proposed rule is intended to clarify and expand existing regulations at 50 CFR 29.32 and defines non-Federal oil and gas development as *"oil and gas activities associated with any private, State, or tribally owned mineral interest where the surface estate is administered by the Service as part of the Refuge System."*

Alaska contains a complex patchwork of land ownership affected by targeted legislation (e.g., Alaska National Interest Land Conservation Act (ANILCA) and the Alaska Native Claims Settlement Act (ANCSA)) that apply unique statutory provisions to non-Federal oil and gas development activities in Alaska. These provisions were put in place to protect the property rights of inholders and accommodate the State's economic and infrastructure needs.

The majority of inholdings within Alaska refuges are not split estate as described in the notice and therefore would not be subject to the proposed rulemaking. While there are limited instances in which such a split estate would be encountered, other laws, regulations and contractual agreements also apply to the various inholdings. Applying additional regulation of oil and gas activities on State and private inholdings in Alaska could impose financial, administrative, and procedural barriers that would be potentially inconsistent and problematic from both a legal and practical standpoint.

The following comments apply generally to all issues identified in the notice but most specifically to the question under Issue 7: *"What unique legislation or legal consideration should the PEIS take into account when analyzing potential impacts on specific regions or States?"*

The Alaska National Interest Lands Conservation Act

In 1980, ANILCA established more than 100 million acres of Federal land in Alaska as new or expanded conservation system units (CSUs). Sixteen refuges comprising 80 million acres are located within Alaska. Due to their vast size, most

CSUs in Alaska contain or effectively surround numerous State and private inholdings, including lands owned by Alaska Native corporations pursuant to ANCSA. Congress incorporated Title XI of ANILCA specifically to ensure that inholders would be guaranteed adequate and feasible access to their lands for economic and other purposes and to further Alaskan's ability to develop the State's fledgling economy and infrastructure. ANILCA provides separate statutory authority, specific to Alaska, which pertains to oil and gas development of non-Federal lands within the boundaries of national wildlife refuges.

ANILCA Section 1101 specifies that ANILCA is the *"single, comprehensive statutory authority"* for approval of transportation and utility systems, including oil and gas development and distribution systems, in Alaska:

> *Congress finds that—(a) Alaska's transportation and utility network is largely undeveloped and the future needs for transportation and utility systems in Alaska would best be identified and provided for through an orderly continuous decisionmaking process involving the State and Federal Governments and the public; (b) the existing authorities to approve or disapprove application for transportation and utility systems through public lands in Alaska are diverse, dissimilar, and, in some cases, absent; and (c) to minimize the adverse impacts of siting transportation and utility systems within units established or expanded by this Act and to insure the effectiveness of the decisionmaking process, **a single comprehensive statutory authority** for the approval or disapproval of applications for such systems must be provided in this Act.* [Emphasis added]

ANILCA Section 1110(b) explicitly protects access by State and private landowners, including owners of subsurface rights underlying public lands, for exploration and development purposes:

> *Notwithstanding any other provisions of this Act or other law, in any case in which State owned or privately owned land, **including subsurface rights of such owners underlying public lands,** or a valid mining claim or other valid occupancy is within or is effectively surrounded by one or more conservation system units, national recreation areas, national conservation areas, or those public lands designated as wilderness study, the State or private owner or occupier **shall be given** by the Secretary **such rights as may be necessary to assure adequate and feasible access for economic and other purposes** to the concerned land by such State or private owner or occupier and their successors in interest. Such rights shall be subject to reasonable regulations issued by the Secretary to protect the natural and other values of such lands.* [Emphasis added]

ANILCA Section 1111(a) secures temporary access across conservation system units for resource exploration and other temporary use by State or private owners:

> *IN GENERAL.—Notwithstanding any other provision of this Act or other law the Secretary **shall authorize and permit** temporary access by the State or a private landowner to or across any conservation system unit, national recreation area, national conservation area, the National Petroleum Reserve—Alaska or those public lands designated as wilderness study or managed to maintain the wilderness character or potential thereof, in order to permit the State or private landowner access to its land **for purposes of survey geophysical, exploratory, or other temporary uses** thereof whenever he determines such access will not result in permanent harm to the resources of such unit, area, Reserve or lands.*

ANILCA Section 1109 specifically preserves all valid existing rights of access:

> *Nothing in this title shall be construed to adversely affect any valid existing right of access.''*

ANILCA Section 103(c) specifically excludes State and private inholdings from Alaska CSUs, and prohibits application of public lands regulation to them. ''Land'' as defined in ANILCA Section 102(1) includes ''lands, waters and interests therein.''

> *Only those lands within the boundaries of any conservation system unit which are public lands (as such term is defined in this Act) shall be deemed to be included as a portion of such unit. **No lands** which, before, on or after the date of enactment of this Act, are conveyed to the State, to any Native Corporation, or to any private party **shall be subject to the regulations applicable solely to public lands within such units.*** [Emphasis added]

State and private inholdings are therefore not part of national wildlife refuges in Alaska, even though such inholdings fall within refuge external boundaries. State and private inholdings are therefore not subject to CSU-specific regulation.

Section 9(b) of the National Wildlife Refuge System Improvement Act of 1977 also supports the applicability of ANILCA to Alaska refuges:

> *Conflicts of Laws—**if any conflict arises** between any provision of this Act and any provision of the Alaska National Interest Lands Conservation Act, then the **provisions of the Alaska National Interest Lands Conservation Act shall prevail.*** [Emphasis added]

NPS Exemption for Alaska

Under Issue 1, the notice asks readers to consider whether National Park Service (NPS) regulations should be used as a model for managing oil and gas resources on refuge lands. In 1981, the NPS promulgated implementing regulations at 36 CFR 13.10–13.16, which recognized these important ANILCA provisions, and explicitly negated the applicability of 36 CFR 9B in Alaska. As stated in the Section-by-Section Analysis (46 FR 31845) of the final rule:

> *Section 13.15(d)(2) is an interpretive rule stating the Department's views that the regulations of 36 CFR Part 9B are no longer applicable in Alaska park areas. These regulations concerning the development of non-Federal oil and gas rights in parks were premised on the land manager's discretion to restrict access. **Section 1110(b) of ANILCA effectively removes this discretion from the land manager. Therefore, 36 CFR Part 9B does not apply to Alaska park areas.*** [Emphasis added]

The final regulation at 36 CFR 13.15(d)(2) stated:

> *Non-Federal Oil and Gas Rights and 36 CFR Subpart 9B. Since Section 1110(b) of ANILCA guarantees adequate and feasible access to park area inholdings notwithstanding any other law, and since 36 CFR Subpart 9B was predicated on the park area Superintendent's discretion to restrict and condition such access, **36 CFR Subpart 9B is no longer applicable in Alaska park areas.*** [Emphasis added]

When the Department of Interior adopted final Title XI regulations at 43 CFR 36 on September 4, 1986 (51 FR 31629), 36 CFR 13.10 through 13.16 were repealed and 43 CFR 36 became the sole regulatory authority governing access to all non-Federal inholdings within CSUs in Alaska (including refuges). This is confirmed in the Section-by-Section analysis for 36 CFR 36.10 ''Access to Inholdings'' (51 FR 31624):

> *Section 36.10(b) has been modified slightly to correct an error in drafting the proposed regulation. The change clarifies that this part is to address all access issues in CSUs, and it was incorrect to also refer to ''other applicable law.''*

For these same reasons, the Service's revised regulations need to also exempt Alaska.

The Alaska Native Claims Settlement Act

ANCSA was enacted to settle aboriginal land claims in Alaska. ANCSA established 12 regional corporations and over 200 village corporations to facilitate the transference of land entitlement allocations via patents to Federal lands. Non-Federal oil and gas ownership in Alaska refuges is largely the result of patents issued pursuant to ANCSA as well as subsequent land exchanges and other legal agreements, such as the 1975 settlement with Cook Inlet Region, Inc. ANCSA § 22(g) addressed the opportunity given to village corporations to select lands within existing refuges as part of their entitlement, with certain conditions:

> *If a patent is issued to any Village Corporation for land in the National Wildlife Refuge System, the patent shall reserve to the United States the right of first refusal if the land is ever sold by the Village Corporation. Notwithstanding any other provision of this Act, every patent issued by the Secretary pursuant to this Act which covers lands lying within the boundaries of a National Wildlife Refuge on the date of enactment of this Act shall contain a provision that such lands remain subject to the laws and regulations governing use and development of such Refuge.*

Not all Native-owned lands within refuge boundaries are subject to ANCSA § 22(g). The provision in those affected patents which provides that lands will be subject to the same laws and regulations governing use and development of the surrounding refuge has been more specifically defined through implementation and related regulations and policies. For example, the preamble to the final compatibility regulations (65 FR 62464) provided a detailed discussion of how Alaska refuges generally manage inholdings subject to ANCSA § 22(g), recognizing their status as private lands:

> [W]hile the plain reading of ANCSA requires all refuge laws and regulations to apply to 22(g) lands, we have historically maintained that the compatibility requirement is the most basic legal requirement to protect refuge lands against uses that materially interfere with refuges achieving their purposes. We have never proposed to apply any other legal standard to uses of 22(g) lands.
>
> We have . . . clarified specifically how compatibility is to apply to 22(g) lands based on substantial comments.. . . These clarifications are substantial and, while recognizing that 22(g) lands are subject to compatibility review, acknowledge that 22(g) lands are also private lands that deserve special attention. We believe we have the authority to adopt regulations that address compatibility differently from those that deal with our own lands because we are, in effect, stating how we are going to implement and require compliance with a provision in a patent.

The final rule at 50 CFR 25.21(b)(1) implements this intent by including numerous limitations on evaluating compatibility for uses of lands subject to ANCSA § 22(g). For example, the Refuge Manager must complete a compatibility determination within 90 days of receiving a request from the landowner (50 CFR 25.21(b)(1)(i)); consultation and an appeal process are provided (50 CFR 25.21(b)(1)(i), (iv)); only effects to adjacent refuge lands (not effects on the § 22(g) lands) and the ability of the refuge to achieve its statutory purposes will be evaluated (50 CFR 25.21(b)(1)(v)).

The regulations also state that a Special Use Permit will not be required for compatible uses of §22(g) lands; noting that special conditions to insure compatibility are to be instead included in the compatibility determination (50 CFR 25.21(b)(1)(viii)). The preamble (65 FR 62466) notes that:

> The commenters stated their desire that proposed uses of 22(g) lands not be subject to the Service's permitting system. We accept this. The final rule states that we will require no additional permits for uses of 22(g) lands beyond the completion of a compatibility determination by the Refuge Manager that finds the use to be compatible with refuge purposes. Any conditions necessary to ensure a proposed use is compatible may be included in the compatibility determination.

Conclusion

Each of the unique and well-established authorization processes applicable to non-Federal oil and gas exploration and development within Alaska refuges was specifically developed to provide for the Alaska context while protecting refuge resources. These existing processes already ensure robust and defensible decisionmaking.

Efforts to accommodate the Alaska regulatory framework within the proposed rule would add unnecessary complexity to the rulemaking effort. The possibility for inadvertent omissions is also likely, potentially creating an untenable legal situation for Alaska refuges, the State, and private property owners.

We therefore request the revised regulations include an exemption for Alaska refuges because existing Department of Interior ANILCA Title XI implementing regulations at 43 CFR Part 36 and Service compatibility regulations at 50 CFR 25.21 for ANCSA 22(g) lands are the applicable regulatory authorities for non-Federal oil and gas development activities occurring within refuges in Alaska.

Sincerely,

SUSAN MAGEE,
ANILCA Program Coordinator.

NATIONAL WILDLIFE REFUGE SYSTEM
OIL AND GAS ACTIVITIES

STATE	OIL&GAS WELLS	PIPELINES
ALASKA	80	7
ALABAMA	14	4
ARKANSAS	---	25
ARIZONA	---	14
CALIFORNIA	25	24
COLORADO	---	7
FLORIDA	---	1
GEORGIA	---	1
IOWA	---	6
ILLINOIS	---	8
INDIANA	15	7
KANSAS	6	9
KENTUCKY	---	3
LOUISIANA	**1150**	130
MASSACHUSETTS	---	2
MICHIGAN	1	1
MINNESOTA	---	8
MISSISSIPPI	13	16
MONTANA	35	2
NORTH CAROLINA	---	3
NEW JERSEY	---	6
NEW MEXICO	13	6
NEW YORK	---	5
NEVADA	---	1
NORTH DAKOTA	1	--
OHIO	---	1
OKLAHOMA	158	9
OREGON	---	4
PENNSYLVANIA	---	8
SOUTH CAROLINA	---	3
TENNESSEE	---	1
TEXAS	167	**153**
UTAH	1	2
VIRGINIA	---	2
WASHINGTON	---	4
WISCONSIN	---	2
WEST VIRGINIA	---	2
WYOMING	---	4
TOTALS	**1,670**	**484**

**NATIONAL WILDLIFE REFUGE SYSTEM UNITS
CLOSED TO THE PUBLIC**

STATES	REFUGE	ESTABLISHED
ALABAMA	FERN CAVE NWR	1981
	SAUTA CAVE NWR	1978
ARKANSAS	LOGAN CAVE NWR	1939
CALIFORNIA	ANTIOCH DUNES NWR	1980
	BITTER CREEK NWR	1985
	BLUE RIDGE NWR	1982
	BUTTE SINK WMA	1980
	CASTLE ROCK NWR	1979
	ELLIOTT SLOUGH NWR	1975
	FARALLON NWR	1909
	HOPPER MOUNTAIN NWR	1974
	MARIN ISLANDS NWR	1992
	NORTH CENTAL VALLEY WMA	1980
	SEAL BEACH NWR	2001
	TULARE BASIN WMA	2010
	WILLOW CREEK-LURLINE WMA	1980
COLORADO	BACA NWR	2000
	COLORADO RIVER WMA	
	ROCKY FLATS NWR	1972
	ROCKY MOUNTAIN FRONT CONSERVATION AREA	2005
	SANGRE de CRISTO CONSERVATION AREA	2012
FLORIDA	CALOOSAHATCHEE NWR	1920
	CROCODILE LAKE NWR	1980
	EVERGLADES HEADWATERS	2012
	ISLAND BAY NWR	1908
	LAKE WALES RIDGE NWR	1993
	MATLACHA PASS NWR	1908
	PASSAGE KEY NWR	1905

	PINE ISLAND NWR		1908
	PINELLAS NWR		1951
	ST. JOHN'S NWR	1971	
GEORGIA	WOLF ISLAND NWR		1930
HAWAII	BAKER ISLAND NWR		1974
	HANALEI NWR		1972
	HAWAIIAN ISLANDS NWR		1909
	HOWLAND ISLAND NWR		1974
	HULE'IA NWR		1973
	JARVIS ISLAND NWR		1974
	JOHNSTON ISLAND NWR		1926
	KAKAHIA NWR	1977	
	KINGMAN REEF NWR	2001	
	MARIANA ARC OF FIRE NWR		2009
	MARIANA TRENCH NWR		2009
	OAHU FOREST NWR		2000
	PEARL HARBOR NWR	1972	
	ROSE ATOLL NWR		1973
ILLINOIS	HACKMATACK NWR		2012
KANSAS	FLINT HILLS LEGACY CONSERVATION AREA		2011
LOUISIANA	SHELL KEYS NWR		1907
MARYLAND	MARTIN NWR		1954
	SUSQUEHANNA NWR		1978
MAINE	SEAL ISLAND NWR		1972
MASSACHUSETTS	MASHPEE NWR		1995
	MASSASOIT NWR		1983
	NOMANS LAND ISLAND NWR		1998
MICHIGAN	DETROIT RIVER INTERNATIONAL NWR		2001

	MICHIGAN ISLANDS NWR	1943
MINNESOTA	MILLE LACS NWR	1915
	TAMARAC WMD	1987
MISSISSIPPI	THEODORE ROOSEVELT NWR	2004
MISSOURI	OZARK CAVEFISH NWR	1991
	PILOT KNOB NWR	1987
MONTANA	LAKE THIBADEAU NWR	1937
	LAMESTEER NWR	1942
	SWAN VALLEY CONSERVATION AREA	2012
NEBRASKA	JOHN W. AND LOUISE SEIER NWR	1999
NEVADA	ANAHO ISLAND NWR	1940
NEW MEXICO	RIO MORA NWR	2012
	SAN ANDRES NWR	1971
NEW YORK	CONSCIENCE POINT NWR	1971
	SEATUCK NWR	1968
NORTH DAKOTA	APPERT LAKE NWR	1939
	ARDOCH NWR	1939
	BONE HILL NWR	1939
	BRUMBA NWR	1939
	BUFFALO LAKES NWR	1939
	CAMP LAKE NWR	1939
	CANFIELD LAKE NWR	1939
	COTTON WOOD LAKE NWR	1939
	DAKOTA LAKE NWR	1939
	DAKOTA TALL GRASS PRARIE	2000
	DAKOTA GRASSLAND CONSERVATION AREA	2011
	HALF-WAY LAKE NWR	1939
	HIDDENWOOD NWR	1939

	HUTCHINSON LAKE NWR	1939
	JOHNSON LAKE NWR	1939
	LAKE GEORGE NWR	1939
	LAKE OTIS NWR	1935
	LAKE PATRICIA NWR	1939
	LAMBS LAKE NWR	1939
	LITTLE GOOSE NWR	1939
	LORDS LAKE NWR	1939
	LOST LAKE NWR	1939
	MAPLE RIVER NWR	1939
	MCLEAN NWR	1939
	NORTH DAKOTA WMA	1939
	PLEASANT LAKE NWR	1939
	PRETTY ROCK NWR	1941
	RABB LAKE NWR	1937
	ROCK LAKE NWR	1939
	ROSE LAKE NWR	1935
	SCHOOL SECTION LAKE NWR	1939
	SHELL LAKE NWR	1939
	SHEYENNE LAKE NWR	1935
	SILVER LAKE NWR	1939
	SNYDER LAKE NWR	1939
	SPRINGWATER LAKE NWR	1939
	STEWART LAKE NWR	1939
	STONEY SLOUGH NWR	1939
	STORM LAKE NWR	1939
	STUMP LAKE NWR	1905
	SUNBURST LAKE NWR	1941
	TOMAHAWK NWR	1939
	WHITE LAKE NWR	1939
	WILD RICE LAKE NWR	1936
	WILLOW LAKE NWR	1939
	WINTERING RIVER NWR	1941
	WOOD LAKE NWR	1936
OHIO	WEST SISTER ISLAND NWR	1937
OKLAHOMA	OZARK PLATEAU NWR	1995
OREGON	BEAR VALLEY NWR	1978
	THREE ARCH ROCKS NWR	1907

	SILETZ BAY NWR	1991
SOUTH CAROLINA	TYBEE NWR	1938
SOUTH DAKOTA	LACREEK WMD	1935
	KARL E. MUNDT NWR	1974
TEXAS	LITTLE SANDY NWR	1986
	MOODY NWR	
	NECHES RIVER NWR	2006
VIRGINIA	FISHERMAN ISLAND NWR	1973
	NANSEMOND NWR	1973
	PLUM THREE ISLAND NWR 1972	
WASHINGTON	COPALIS NWR	1907
	FLATTERY ROCKS NWR	1907
	FRANZ LAKE NWR	1990
	PIERCE NWR	1983
	PROTECTION ISLAND NWR 1982	
	QUILLAYUTE NEEDLES NWR	1907
WISCONSIN	FOX RIVER NWR	1979
	GRAVEL ISLAND NWR	1915
	GREEN BAY NWR	2007
WYOMING	BAMFORTH NWR	1932
	COKEVILLE MEADOWS NWR	1993
	MORTENSON LAKE NWR	1992
PUERTO RICO	DESECHEO NWR	1976
	NAVASSA ISLAND NWR	1999
VIRGIN ISLANDS	GREEN CAY NWR	1977

TOTAL NUMBER OF CLOSED UNITS = 147 (October 23, 2013)
TOTAL NUMBER OF CLOSED UNITS = 88 (May 2005)

www.ingramcontent.com/pod-product-compliance
Lightning Source LLC
Chambersburg PA
CBHW080831180526
45168CB00006B/2645